MANCHESTER
VICTORIA
STATION

TOM WRAY

PETER TAYLOR PUBLICATIONS . HEREFORD

The **Lancashire & Yorkshire Railway** *Society*

Frontispiece: *Probably the most familiar view of Victoria station when approaching from the centre of Manchester is the corner containing the clock tower and on which, even today can still be seen the legend "Lancashire & Yorkshire Railway".*
National Railway Museum

Right: *One of the distinctive features on Victoria Station Approach was the canopy along the pavement which was decorated with many of the destinations served by the LYR either directly or indirectly, over other railway companies or by the company owned steamers to Ireland or the Continent.*

Opposite: *J.A.F. Aspinall's overhead parcels carrier shown traversing over platforms 11 and 12 with the electric motored drive clearly shown running along the top of the track held by the stirupped suspension rods.*

Designed by: Peter Taylor
Printed by: Circle Services Ltd

Published by:
Peter Taylor Publications
Hereford + The L&YR Society

CONTENTS

THE EARLY YEARS

ORIGINS + NEGOTIATIONS   1

CLEARANCE + NEW STATION   8

EARLY OPERATION +
THE LNWR   18

HEAD OFFICE +
CEMETARY EXTENSION   21

TOWARDS MATURITY

SIDINGS, SHEDS +
FISH MARKET   27

STATION EXTENSIONS +
SALFORD LINE   30

WORKHOUSE ACQUISITION
+PLATFORM DEVELOPMENTS   36

MATURITY ACCOMPLISHED

ELECTRIC LIGHTING +
CARRIAGE STORAGE   55

EXCHANGE STATION +
LNWR DEVELOPMENTS   59

PARCELS OFFICE +
CARRIER   64

STATION EXTENSIONS   73

SIGNALLING +
CENTRAL CONTROL   92

20th CENTURY ASPECTS

ELECTRIFICATION +
THEN WAR   103

RELATIONS BETWEEN THE
LYR +LNWR   112

20th CENTURY ASPECTS   120

CHANGES, DECLINE +
METROLINK   122

INTRODUCTION

The first suggestion for the extension of the Manchester and Leeds Railway to join another from the Liverpool and Manchester Railway at a central station in Hunts Bank, Manchester came from one John Macfarlane. His idea, relegated to a mere footnote in Butterworth's descriptive history which introduced A.F. Tait's Views on the Manchester and Leeds railway, would have consequences unimagined at the time.

The station, opened in 1844, would not only cater for the travelling public but would also become the administrative centre of the railway company which would expand from fifty route miles in 1844 to 601 miles when the amalgamation of the LYR and the LNWR took place in 1921. At that time the company owned 1,650 locomotives, 3,776 carriages, 67,500 wagons, with 45 miles of electrified railway and also thirty-three revenue earning ships, several of which were jointly owned with the LNWR.

In roughly twenty year stages Victoria station would be extended from a single platform to one having seventeen platforms with no less than twenty five roads stretching from south to north which included platform roads, sidings and through lines, making it one of the largest stations in the kingdom outside London. With the final extensions completed in the first decade of the twentieth century the station remained almost intact until the last decade.

Though it is difficult to pin down an accurate figure for the number of trains using the station a typical winter timetable shortly after the formation of the LMSR would include 390 trains arriving and 370 leaving the station with an increase of about sixty trains during the summer but this does not take into account the number of excursions, reliefs and duplicates nor indeed the goods trains which passed through the station. To deal with over half a million passengers arriving at and leaving the station each week there were at this time over 400 railway staff ranging from the station master to the junior cloakroom attendant.

This history of Victoria station has depended considerably on reports and articles in the archives of the Manchester Guardian and other newspapers which are held on microfilm in Manchester Central Library together with technical journals such as The Engineer, Engineering, Railway Engineer and several others.

First published in five short articles in Platform the journal of the Lancashire and Yorkshire Railway Society this history has been extended as further research has revealed more information though the author accepts that it is probably not complete and he also takes full responsibility for any mistakes that it may contain.

THE
EARLY
YEARS

The opening, on 1 January 1844, of Victoria station by the Manchester and Leeds Railway Company marked the culmination of several years of frustration and negotiation, for, from the inception of the scheme to join three railways in Manchester, one of the parties repeatedly offered alternatives and objections. The scheme originated in 1838 when the Manchester and Leeds Railway realised the importance of direct communication between the railways that entered Manchester from east and west and proposed a junction railway from Miles Platting to a central station and on through Salford to a junction with the Liverpool and Manchester Railway making use of a section of the Manchester, Bolton and Bury Railway.

The Manchester and Leeds Railway Company had been formed in 1836 to construct a railway from Oldham Road, Manchester through Rochdale, Todmorden and Wakefield to Leeds. Construction of the railway had commenced in August 1837 and almost two years later the first section was opened between Manchester and Littleborough. The viaduct on which the terminus at Manchester was built carried the railway to Collyhurst Lane where a round house for locomotives was erected on the north side of the line and it was from near this location that the company proposed to make a junction for the new railway to a

site adjacent to the Manchester Union Workhouse close to Hunts Bank.

In July 1838 the Leeds company approached the Liverpool and Manchester Railway company with details of the proposal. Soon afterwards the Liverpool company directors reported favourably to their proprietors the "desirableness of a connecting railway" between the two companies and that the proposition would receive the "best consideration and attention of the Board".

By the September of 1838 the Liverpool company entered negotiations with the Manchester, Bolton and Bury Railway Company over whose railway part of the extension was to pass. As initially envisaged the extension line in Salford was to leave the Manchester to Liverpool railway east of Cross Lane and join the Bolton railway west of Oldfield Road. From the New Bailey Street terminus the Bolton company were to extend their railway to Hunts Bank there to join the Manchester and Leeds Railway extension from Miles Platting. The Liverpool company were not too happy with the involvement of the Bolton company, preferring to build the western section themselves. Nonetheless an agreement was reached between the two companies which entailed the use of about half a mile of the Bolton railway and that that company would lay a third line of rails and keep a

least two lines open day and night. For the use of this section of railway the Liverpool company would pay a toll of $1^3/_4$d per passenger and 6d per ton of goods, there were to be no tolls for parcels, horses or carriages. In the event of the Liverpool company raising their fares the Bolton company would receive one penny per passenger for every six pence of the increase. On their part the Bolton company were prevented, by a clause on the agreement, from becoming part of a competing line to Liverpool.

A special meeting of the Leeds company, held on 17 January 1839, resolved to apply to Parliament for powers to make the extension to Hunt Bank and to build a central station there. The Leeds company proposed that the two main companies agree to complete the extension within two years, however, the Liverpool company stated that they could not enter such an agreement; they also requested more detailed estimates of the traffic expected on the extension. In this the Leeds company were at a distinct disadvantage for their railway was still as yet unfinished, so the estimates advanced were based on those formulated for presentation to Parliament in 1836. The Liverpool company intimated that some of their proprietors had been pressing for more definite information and this, followed by a letter to the Leeds company from a

1

Left: The early provision of company offices was enabled by covering over the river Irk and re-siting Walkers Croft above the river. By further extensions Walkers Croft completely covered the river as far as Victoria Station Approach. Agreement to cover the river had been made with Chethams College whose property flanked the southern bank.

Below: The nucleus of Manchester is readily seen from this early illustration of the town showing the distinctive street pattern which survives to the present day. From the Collegiate Church streets such as Deansgate, Market Street, Withy Grove and Long Millgate are recognised together with the sweep of the river Irwell flowing from the right and beneath Victoria Bridge. The community of Salford, on the north bank of the Irwell, is concentrated in the region of Chapel Street, Greengate and Gravel Lane with Trinity Church at the far end. From the bottom the river Irk passes beneath Scotland Bridge at the foot of Red Bank then curves under Tanners and Mill Brow bridges to Hunts Bank Bridge where it flows into the Irwell. The railway will eventually pass from the bottom centre of the picture diagonally to the upper right hand corner.

representative of the Bridgewater Trustees' interests in the Liverpool company drawing attention to an alternative junction railway to the south of Manchester which would be cheaper and more beneficial to the general public, gave the Leeds company reason to suspect that pressure was being put on the Liverpool company to consider the southern junction in preference to the northern line.

The Bridgewater Trust was established on the death of the third Duke of Bridgewater, the Canal Duke, in 1803. In a complex will made by the Duke the Trust was formed for the benefit of his nephew, George Granville Leveson-Gower, Marquess of Stafford and later the first Duke of Sutherland, during his lifetime and then to his second son, Francis, on the condition that he adopt the name Egerton. By the time Lord Francis Egerton assumed control, in 1837, the Trust was a powerful and influential body employing about 3,000 people, selling 273,000 tons of coal annually and carrying just short of 1,000,000 tons of goods on the Bridgewater Canal each year. When, in 1822, the construction of a railroad between Liverpool and Manchester was proposed the opposition of the Trustees was sufficient to delay its progress. The curious decision, in 1825, by the Marquess of Stafford to invest £100,000 in the Liverpool and Manchester Railway caused the opposition of the Trustees to the railway scheme to evaporate. The investment included the power to nominate three of the fifteen directors on the board of the railway. Until the death of

the Marquess of Stafford in 1833 James Lock had been his principal agent since 1812, a position which he retained to the heir who inherited the interest in the Liverpool and Manchester Railway and to the second son who inherited the interest in the Bridgewater Trust, Lock also became superintendent of the Trust in 1837, and for a period was a director of the Liverpool company board. The considerable community of interest in the relationship between the railway and the canal companies placed Lock in a curious but powerful position.

Inspite of the Bridgewater lobby the Liverpool company proceeded with their application to Parliament for the Act for the extension to Hunts Bank which was granted on 14 June 1839, the Leeds company Act was granted on 1 July, three days before that company opened the first section of their railway between Manchester and Littleborough.

The hesitant attitude of the Liverpool company prompted the Leeds company to inquire, in February 1840, of the Mersey and Irwell Navigation Company whether the river Irwell could be made navigable up to Hunts Bank This company, known popularly as the Old Quay Company, had existed since 1721 when it was authorised to make the rivers Mersey and Irwell navigable as far as Hunts Bank, Manchester. In the event, the upper limit of the navigation was established at Quay Street, half a mile short of Hunts Bank. Over the years the navigation company had become a thorn in the side of the Bridgewater Trustees because of its cursory attitude

toward the maintenance of rates, agreements and the partition of traffic between Liverpool and Manchester. The opportunism of the Old Quay company was exploited by the Leeds company as a means to persuade the Liverpool company from its lethargic approach to the Hunts Bank extension scheme.

By September 1840 the lack of progress on the junction railway was giving cause for much concern to the Leeds company. The proprietors were told that the directors were unable to explain the attitude of the Liverpool company but they felt that the powers granted to the company should not be allowed to lapse and that they should proceed with their part of the extension. In the following month the Leeds company noted that the river Irwell had been made navigable to Victoria Bridge, just short of Hunts Bank.

The half yearly meeting of the Leeds company held in September 1841 was told that the extension railway had been delayed not only by the inactivity of the Liverpool company but also because of the economic climate and the reluctance, by the directors, to commit the shareholders to any major capital expenditure during the period of the depression. They felt, however, that some positive decision was unavoidable because the parliamentary powers to purchase land for the junction line would expire in July 1842. The meeting was also told that since the railway had been opened throughout on the 1 of March 1841 the lack of positive traffic returns had been eliminated.

The Leeds company, at this meeting, resolved to proceed with land purchase and, if the Liverpool company continued their opposition, to make a communication with the Mersey and Irwell Navigation, an arrangement with which the directors were not happy, feeling it to be inferior to direct rail communication.

An agreement was, in fact, reached between the Leeds company and the Mersey and Irwell Navigation Company in February 1842 to carry between Hull and Liverpool. The Leeds company appear to have entered this agreement as a way of getting at the Bridgewater Trustees who they felt were responsible for the failure of the Liverpool company to build their extension to Hunts Bank. The Old Quay Company, however, reported to the Trustees that they had not intended any exclusive agreement with the Leeds company who promptly deserted the navigation company.

Then, in January 1842, the Liverpool company reported that they had not proceeded with their part of the junction railway because they believed that it would be unlikely to prove remunerative. The Leeds company resolved to guarantee the Liverpool company an annual dividend of 10 per cent for a term of years on the total capital of that company and a similar rate upon the cost of the western section of the junction railway if it were completed forthwith. Predictably the proposal was rejected at a general meeting of the Liverpool company held on 26 January. It was significant that, at this meeting, though the directors

recommended the abandonment of the extension to Hunts Bank they stated that the ultimate decision should be delayed until a special meeting was called when further information regarding the southern junction line would be put before the proprietors. The reasons for the recommendation to abandon the extension hinged on several points but mainly that there was not enough satisfactory information given by the Leeds company regarding the estimates of traffic likely over the junction line; that, unbeknown to them, the Manchester and Birmingham Railway Company were actively interested in making a junction between their terminus in Store Street to the Manchester and Leeds Railway at Hunts Bank; and they accused the Manchester, Bolton and Bury Company of demanding extortionate terms from them, the Liverpool company, for passing over the Bolton railway.

The Bolton company were, quite naturally, outraged at this last accusation and issued a statement denying that they were responsible for demanding unacceptable terms from the Liverpool company, they added that as far as they were aware there was no discussion when the Bill was before Parliament on the agreement made between the two companies and that the Liverpool company had made no intimation of any dissatisfaction with the agreement since that date until the publication of the report of their meeting held on 26 January.

Early in February 1842 the Liverpool company gave notice of an application to Parliament

for powers to build a railway to the south of Manchester from their railway near Liverpool Road to the Manchester and Birmingham Railway in Store Street. Several years earlier a similar railway scheme, the Manchester Connexion Railway, had been promoted but was defeated by the powerful Bridgewater Trustees over whose land the railway would have mainly passed. Ironically it was the same Trustees who now used their influence within the Liverpool company to support the southern junction. Support in the venture was sought from the Birmingham company but they declined, for financial reasons, to become involved, instead they pledged their support for the junction between Store Street and the Leeds company at Hunts Bank. This latter connecting line got no further than the preliminary planning stage and was probably the first of several attempts over many decades to provide Manchester with an underground railway to connect with surface railways.

From the Birmingham railway at Store Street which was carried on a viaduct, hoists would descend about 67 feet to a tunnel capable of carrying two railway lines. Tunnelling in a north-westerly direction it would have passed beneath the Ashton and Rochdale canals, Port Street, Stevenson Square and Shudehill before coming to the surface to the north of Long Millgate and cross the river Irk before reaching the Hunts Bank station. It was intended that there would be 1,539 yards of tunnel, the greater portion of which would be on a gradient of 1 in 1,124, falling towards

Hunts Bank. Estimates for the work were £66,500 and it was agreed that should the railway be built the Leeds company would withdraw from all competition with the Birmingham company for traffic between Manchester and London. Whether the Leeds Company intentionally deceived the Birmingham company is difficult to ascertain but almost as soon as the Liverpool company agreed to build their part of the northern extension the Leeds company appeared to lose interest in the tunnel scheme. In reply to protests from the Birmingham company the Leeds company claimed that the M & B intended to flout the terms of the agreement of non-competition between the two companies for certain traffic and that the plans for the tunnel had not been advertised by the Birmingham company but by a new company under the title of the Manchester and Birmingham Junction Railway. The Leeds company felt that they were not obliged to grant the new company the same advantages as to the Birmingham company. The latter retorted that the Leeds company were willing to accept their support and they denied all the allegations which had been made, feeling that the Leeds company had behaved dishonourably. And there the matter rested.

At the special meeting of the Liverpool company on 15 March 1842 the directors expressed their desire to continue to negotiate amicably with the Leeds company whilst at the same time to proceed with plans for the southern junction railway. They reiterated their

opposition to the Hunts Bank scheme, the tunnel, and the suggested buyout of their company by the Leeds company, they also suggested that the question of the best scheme for connecting the railways in Manchester should be the subject of arbitration.

In reply the MLR directors meeting on the 17 March reasserted their intention to proceed with their part of the extension. They rejected the suggestion of arbitration on the grounds that any decision could not be reached before the parliamentary powers had lapsed. The directors reported that a letter had been received from Charles Lawrence, the chairman of the Liverpool company, suggesting that there be an amicable meeting of the chairman of both companies to try to devise a means of settling the differences which existed. It was significant that the Liverpool chairman would be accompanied by George Loch, one of the Duke of Sutherland's nominee directors and also the son of James Loch of the Bridgewater Trustees. Such a meeting was sanctioned by the MLR proprietors on the condition that the parliamentary powers were not jeopardised. It was also revealed that the estimated cost of building a connecting railway from Hunts Bank to the Bolton railway terminus in New Bailey Street was about £100,000 and that at a meeting between the Leeds company and representatives of the "northern companies" there was a willingness to contribute towards this cost if negotiations with the Liverpool company broke down.

A month later the Liverpool

company reported that the MLR were intent on completing their line to Hunts Bank and had declined offers of mediation or arbitration. The Liverpool company appeared to realise that if they proceeded with the southern junction it would be without the co-operation of and probably with the hostility of the two companies most imediately connected with the scheme. The chairman intimated that even at this stage it might still be possible to reach agreement with both the Leeds and the Bolton companies for an amended line from Ordsall Lane to the New Bailey Street terminus of the Bolton company and then by the parliamentary line to Hunts Bank. By adopting this revised plan the whole of the junction line from Ordsall Lane to Hunts Bank would be an integral part of the Liverpool and Manchester Railway.

To emphasise their determination to build the railway the Manchester and Leeds Railway Company advertised for tenders for two contracts on the 30 April 1842.

The first contract was for a railway from a point about four chains east of Collyhurst Lane (later Street) to the east side of Lower Tebbutt Street, about 1,516 yards including excavations and embankments, the building of arches over reservoirs at Collyhurst, a bridge over Collyhurst Lane and bridges under Cropper Street and Saint Georges Road (Rochdale Road). Contract two continued from Lower Tebbutt Street to the intended station at Hunts Bank, about 701 yards being mainly of viaduct and bridges and crossing the river Irk three times.

Below + right: *The two maps show the changes between 1794 and 1823 with the earlier illustrating how much of a backwater the Hunts Bank area was before the coming of the railway. By the date of the second map, all the buildings between Hunts Bank and the river Irwell had been demolished and the carriageway widened and improved, Hunts Bank bridge was raised and widened and a new highway, Great Ducie Street, built to replace the meandering Strangeways Walk. A new bridge over the river Irwell gave its name to New Bridge Street which then extended past the workhouse to Cheetham Hill Road. Another piece of the jigsaw was the extension of Miller Street over the river Irk at Ducie Bridge to connect with New Bridge Street.*

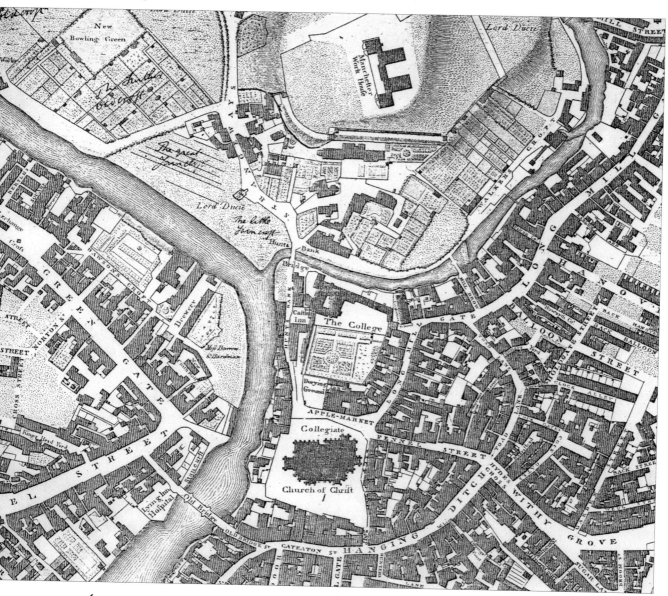

CLEARANCE +
NEW STATION

One of the deciding factors which probably influenced the Manchester and Leeds Railway to choose to project the extension railway to the north of the township of Manchester in 1838 was the fact that little of the land had been built on, even the site which was to be appropriated for the joint station had an almost rural aspect.

At the turn of the nineteenth century vehicular traffic leaving Manchester frequently had to negotiate the narrow confines of Long Millgate, to cross the river Irk at Scotland Bridge and the steep climb at Red Bank before reaching the wider expanses of the old turnpike road through Cheetham Hill to places such as Bury and Rochdale. Some relief was obtained in 1814 when a new road was built as a continuation of Miller Street northward over Long Millgate and the river Irk to the lower end of Cheetham Hill Road, then called York Street, and not fully developed. The bridge over the river was named after its benefactor, Lord Ducie and a toll bar existed at its northern end until 1830. At the beginning of York Street a junction was made with another new street, New Bridge Street, named after, and extended from, a new crossing over the river Irwell at Strangeways. New Bridge Street passed along the north side of the Manchester Union Workhouse which the Guardians of the Poor had had built in 1793 and which was to play a significant

role in the development of Victoria station.

Between Long Millgate and the river Irk from Chethams College to Scotland Bridge there was a high density of industrial and very poor quality residential property which Frederick Engels would write about disparagingly some years later and which contrasted markedly with the open, almost rural area north of the river and Walkers Croft. Between Walkers Croft and the workhouse a parish burial ground had been consecrated by the Bishop of Chester in 1815.

Hunts Bank at this time extended from the Collegiate Church to Hunts Bank bridge over the river Irk beyond which was Strangeways Walk, little more than a footpath which meandered northward before petering out in the open countryside.

Improvements made under an Act of Parliament of 1829 included the extension and rebuilding of Hunts Bank alongside the river Irwell and several feet higher and a new bridge over the river Irk. When completed Hunts Bank extended from Deansgate, at Victoria Bridge Street, to the river Irk from where a completely new road, to be called Great Ducie Street for the first quarter mile and then Bury New Road was built and completed in 1831.

The Leeds company proposed to build their station on land between York Street and the

river Irwell cutting between the workhouse and the burial ground in a north-east to south-west direction.

When a substantial amount of land at the Hunts Bank side of the site came on the market Samuel Brooks, the Leeds company deputy chairman and a banker, took a lease on it on the 1 January 1839. Brooks bought quite an amount of land in and about Manchester; Whalley Range, which he named after his family home, and Sale at Brooklands, were but two of his larger purchases, so when he bought the Hunts Bank land it probably did not raise many eyebrows. He informed his fellow directors that he had purchased the site long before it was contemplated that the station would be built there but if the company required the land they could have it on reasonable terms and he would not sell it until they had decided whether they wanted it or not. In the event, Brooks re-assigned the property to the Manchester and Leeds Railway on the 20 July 1839 for £9,345 and the rest of the 999 year lease at an annual rent of £734-10-0d. A mansion on this land which had been the home of the late Dorothy Clowes and her husband the Reverend Clowes, also deceased, was to become, for a short period at least, the head offices of the Leeds company and was indeed used to hold a special meeting of the company on the 17 January less than three weeks after Brooks had signed the lease. The building was situated behind the Flying Horse Inn in a commanding position at the foot of the workhouse garden. Not letting much grass grow, the Leeds company had already located the secretary's office, the directors board room and other waiting rooms there and on the upper floor two large rooms had been converted into one spacious area for general meetings with a platform at one end for the chairman, managing director and other officials. With an eye to good relations with the press a desk and coat hooks were provided for reporters. This the first meeting to be held there was attended by over fifty proprietors.

The churchwardens and the overseers of the township convened a meeting on the 26 February 1839 to determine what action to take in response to the notice given by the Manchester and Leeds Railway to seek powers to take the property of the workhouse and the burial ground for the extension railway. By the time a second public meeting had been held, on the 9 of May, the churchwardens had discovered that the Leeds company did not intend to take the whole of both properties but only a small portion and certainly they would not disturb any bodies but traverse the burial ground on the surface! A report on the 13 July castigated the church-

wardens for opposing the MLR bill stating that all that had been achieved was a ten foot wall on either side of the railway where it passed through the burial ground and that the Leeds company now had the power to purchase the whole of the land on the south side of the railway and when it was necessary they were to pay for the removal of bodies that relatives had not removed. It went on to state that any advantages achieved might well have been obtained without expense if the churchwardens had chosen to negotiate, as it turned out the leypayers came out of pocket to the tune of £480-14-9d.

By October 1842 some demolition and clearance of the site had taken place and, as it was obvious that the mansion, which housed the company offices, would also have to go so temporary offices at the Oldham Road terminus were arranged. It had also been found that it was necessary to raise the level of the road over the Hunts Bank bridge by four feet and to build an arch over the river Irk for a distance of thirty yards to enable the incline approach to the proposed railway to be built. This roadway, Hunts Bank Approach, ascended at an inclination of 1 in 20 and was fifty feet wide including two eight feet wide footways, with the top to be opposite the centre

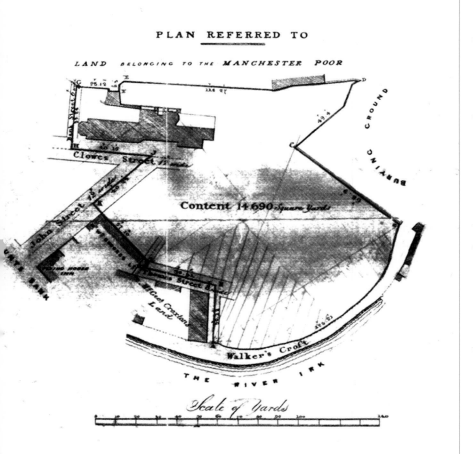

PLAN REFERRED TO

LAND BELONGING TO THE MANCHESTER POOR

Content 14.690 Square Yards

Scale of Yards

Left: *The pocket of land that Samuel Brooks purchased in 1839 would be crucial to the development of Victoria station bound as it was by Walkers Croft, the cemetery and the workhouse. The building at the top left hand corner was most likely to have been that in which the company offices were first located.*

of the station house, the retaining walls on either side would be surmounted with ornamental iron railings.

On 6 March 1843 the tender of John Brogden of £19,000 for the erection of the station at Hunts Bank was accepted, a month earlier the tender of Fox and Henderson & Company of £6,975 was accepted for the iron roof of the station.

The station house, erected on the south side of the railway, was originally a single storey building in stone in the Roman Doric style 266 feet long by 36 feet wide divided equally between the two companies. The central portion of the building, having a frontage of about sixty feet housed the first and second class dining room and the ladies waiting room lit by elegant circular headed windows with stone pilasters. On either side, with entrances recessed beneath covered ways, were the two booking offices and at either ends of the building were the offices and residences of the station masters. From the dining room to the platform were two doors, ostensibly one for Liverpool passengers and one for Leeds passengers, though more than likely they would have been used indiscriminately. On the basement floor, approached from the platform by stone steps, and for the use of the third class passengers, was a coffee room and chop house, fitted upon the London plan(?), with bells to indicate which trains were about to leave. Several years after the station opened these refreshment rooms were advertised in the following manner;

"The public are respectfully informed, that 'hot joints' are always in readiness, from one o'clock until six o'clock in the afternoon, and that the following are the charges; Dinner, from the joint with vegetables and cheese, ls 6d; soup, or fish, or sweets, with dinner, 6d extra; Port or Sherry, 5s per bottle; Ale and Porter on draught or in bottles; Wines, Spirits and etc. of every description, at equally low charges".

In addition to the third class refreshment room the basement contained kitchens, wine and spirit cellars, ale and porter stores, together with general stores and porter's rooms.

The Leeds company divided their booking office into two, one half for first and second class passengers and the other half for third class. The company, from experience, separated the passengers as early as possible due to the great demand in the last few minutes before a train was due to leave, also, on this line there were more third class passengers than the other two classes combined. The Liverpool company appeared to be not too keen on third class passengers, indeed quite a number of trains to Liverpool had no third class accommodation at all for some years. Adjacent to the booking offices was a waiting lobby and conveniences for passengers together with a parcels office.

The single platform which, in front of the station house was twenty four feet wide, extended beyond the end of the building for 184 feet by 12 feet wide westwards and 120 feet by 12 feet wide eastwards with a bay to the south of each platform used as an arrival platform by each company. The line of demarcation between the two companies was marked clearly by two rows of turntables across the five lines in the train shed and two further sidings outside to the north. The Liverpool company had two more rows of turntables in their part of the station but the Leeds company had only one additonal row in their half.

From Great Ducie Street at the west end and for a distance of 700 feet all five lines were covered by an iron roof of three longitudinal spans, the south being 26 feet 3 inches, the centre 59 feet 6 inches and the north span 28 feet. The roof was slated and the underside was lined with boards; skylights, glazed with Chances' patent glass in panes of four feet by one foot, provided adequate lighting during daylight hours. In periods of darkness there were fifteen gas lamps within the station. The gas lights consisted of a number of radiating tubes, like the spokes of a wheel, perforated with holes for the flat flame burners invented by Messrs. Hall's of King Street, Manchester. There was also one large gas lamp opposite the station house and several more on the Hunts Bank Approach. All the gas lamps were connected to a central control enabling maximum illumination when trains arrived or before departure and minimum illumination between times giving a considerable saving. The roof was supported by the station building on the south side, the retaining wall of the workhouse on the north side and by iron columns inside the train shed.

Below: This map of 1850 reveals how decisively the new railway sliced its way between Walkers Croft cemetery and the workhouse property. It also shows the rebuilt Hunts Bank bridge to accommodate the carriageway up to the station and before the river Irk was covered over to provide the space at the foot of Hunts Bank Approach where the company offices would be built. One of the two engine 'houses' built by the LNWR on the west side of the river Irwell stands on what would later be the site of Exchange station. From Long Millgate, Mill Brow leads down to the footbridge over the river Irk which was to be a bone of contention for many years. Note also that from the row of turntables in the MLR part of the station a siding is extended into the workhouse property.

Overleaf: When Victoria station was opened on the 1 January 1844 it was described as being 'the most extensive in the kingdom even surpassing the justly celebrated one at Derby'. However, the limitations of having a single platform was soon to become a serious disadvantage which would be criticised on several occasions not only by the Board of Trade inspectors but also the general public. One thing which could not have been foreseen was the remarkable development of railways and the growth of railway travel within the next few years. A glance at the plan of the station in 1844 reveals many of the inherent problems faced when working trains into and out of the station when there were so many conflicting movements. There were no facilities for engines to run round their trains, indeed, it does not appear that engines were ever intended to enter the station at all. On the LNWR side trains were stopped outside the station and then pushed into the arrival platform having to cross over the departure line in the process. On the LYR side the carriages were allowed to run into the arrival platform by gravity and by the same means when leaving the departure platform, only when outside the station was the engine attached and the bank wagon coupled up to the rear of the train. The number of turntables in the station appears to be a recipe for disaster particularly when placed on the through running lines, however, carriages of the day were only a little longer than goods wagons of later years and it was quite common for carriages to be turned on turntable by the effort of two or three men. In spite of some relatively minor alterations this plan remained the same for many years.

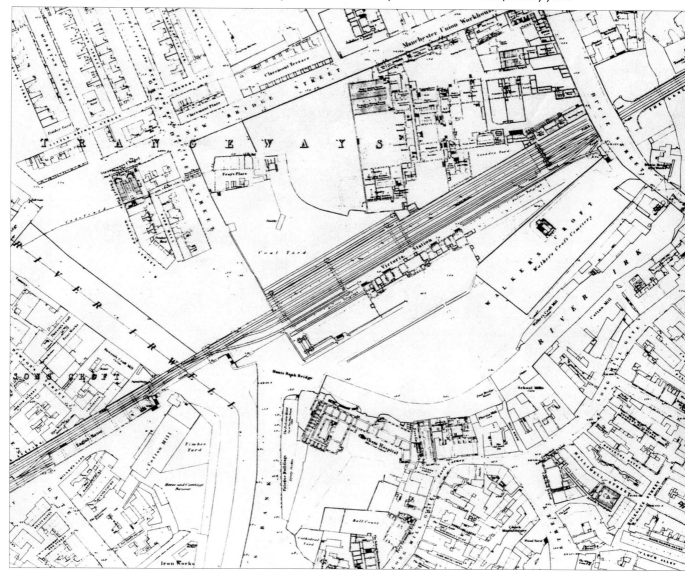

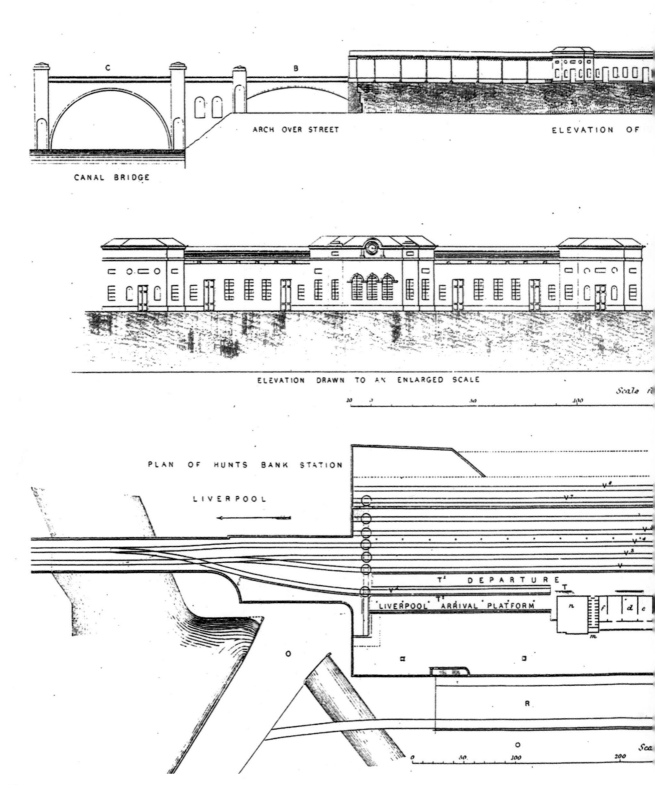

HUNTS BANK JUNCTION STATION OF THE MANCHESTE

CANAL BRIDGE

ARCH OVER STREET

ELEVATION OF

ELEVATION DRAWN TO AN ENLARGED SCALE

Scale f

PLAN OF HUNTS BANK STATION

LIVERPOOL

DEPARTURE

LIVERPOOL ARRIVAL PLATFORM

VERPOOL & THE MANCHESTER & LEEDS RAILWAYS.

UILDINGS & SHEDS

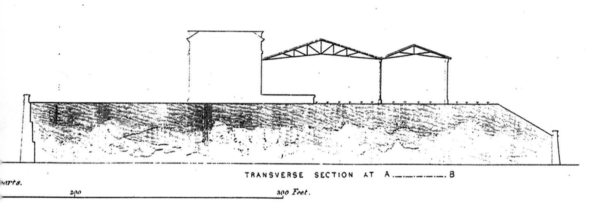

TRANSVERSE SECTION AT A——————B

arts.   200   300 *Feet.*

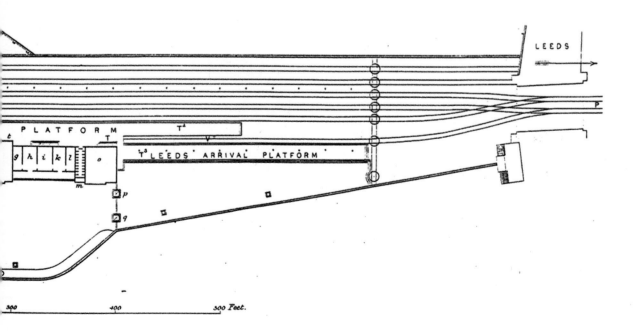

LEEDS

PLATFORM

T⁴

t   T   V

g h i k l   *o*   T³ LEEDS ARRIVAL PLATFORM

m

p

q

P

300   400   500 *Feet.*

Above + below: *Of the two lithographs by A.F. Tait for his collection for the Manchester and Leeds Railway the upper one shows the exterior of the station building and the circulating area at the top of Hunts Bank Approach whilst the lower shows the interior. The LNWR occupied that part of the building leftwards of the clock in the centre with the LYR owning the other half. Though Tait shows a clock face, in fact it was not until 1855 that the company got round to fitting one. Internally, the platform to the left was the single departure platform used by both companies with bays at each end used for arrivals. The two tracks between the platform line and row of roof columns were, in theory, to be used for trains which passed through the station but as can be seen some vehicles have been left on the east bound track. Beyond the columns were two more sidings both to be used for storing carriages out of use. The three carriages in the MLR part of the sidings were special vehicles which had a short life and were not replaced. The lightness of the carriages at this time can be appreciated by the fact that they could easily be moved by two or three men.*

Right: *Surprisingly, almost all the original Hunts Bank station still survives. The most obvious being the main building and the west wing when viewed from Victoria Station Approach. Many years of grime were cleaned off in 1979 to reveal the original stonework although the clock had been removed quite a few years before. The front windows are replicated on the platform side with the barrier protecting steps leading down to what had formerly been a third class refreshment room. When the new office block was completed in 1909 it butted up against the east wing of the older building which is now only visible on the platform side.*

Overleaf: *Although A.F. Tait's illustrations of the Manchester and Leeds railway are well known, the print overleaf was not used in that collection which is unfortunate for it illustrates a fascinating scene from the Salford side of the river Irwell. The steps on the left lead up to the LNWR engine houses whilst on either side of the river bridge can be seen coats of arms, possibly of Manchester and Liverpool and a locomotive can be observed through the bridge railings. It is no doubt a revelation to modern eyes to see rowing boats and other larger craft on the river with a variety of goods being either loaded or unloaded by the larger vessel. Hunts Bank, not re-named Victoria Street until the end of the century, is busy with traffic and pedestrians and a horse 'bus or large carriage is starting to climb the Hunts Bank Approach. The new office building is pristine in its new stone work at the corner of Walkers Croft beneath which the river Irk flows to its confluence with the Irwell. Also looking very smart is the Palatine Hotel built as a speculation by the general manager of the Leeds company, Mr Robert Gill, and in which some of the rooms were used as temporary offices by the MLR The hotel manager, Mr. David Maurigy combined that position with that of station refreshment room manager. A curiosity about the Palatine Hotel was a livery stable on one of the upper floors.*

15

EARLY OPERATION +
THE LNWR

At a special general meeting of the Manchester and Leeds Railway held in offices at the Oldham Road terminus on Thursday, 28 December 1843, one of the proprietors submitted to the chairman a resolution suggesting that the designation of the new station in Manchester should be "The Victoria Station" as the Hunts Bank station did not appear to him, to be appropriate. The resolution, subject to the approval of the Liverpool and Manchester Railway Company, was passed unanimously.

The meeting ended with the chairman inviting those present to join him on the platform upstairs where an engine and carriages were waiting to convey the party to Miles Platting and then along the new railway to Victoria station.

On Friday, 29 December General Pasley made a favourable inspection of the railway, on behalf of the Board of Trade, between Hunts Bank and Newton (Miles Platting) stations.

At 7.00am on New Years Day 1844 without public celebration but to the cheers of those assembled the first train departed from Victoria station and ascended the incline without the assistance of the wire rope which had not been ready in time. The same timetable as that used by the MLR from the Oldham Road terminus applied, supplemented by a half hourly shuttle service from 8.00am to 8.00pm between Victoria and Miles Platting.

Work on the Leeds company extension had been under active construction in September 1842 by which time tenders had been invited for the ancillary plant and machinery required for the operation of the incline with the exception of the buildings to house the stationary engines at Collyhurst and the station building at Hunts Bank.

Work at the top of the incline involved the excavation of a culvert 99 feet long by 19 feet wide and sinking a shaft 90 feet deep by $4^1/_2$ feet in diameter together with the installation of a high pressure marine steam engine which had cylinders of 33 inch diameter and a stroke of 5 feet. Three boilers each with a working pressure of 50lbs per square inch were required and there was also the necessary equipment such as pulleys, wheels, balancing frame and weights and the all important wire rope.

The Liverpool company were much slower off the mark; the company had held a special meeting on the 5 July 1842 to consider the draft of the bill for extending their railway and though the new Act was granted on the 30 July it was not until January 1843 that it was reported that the contracts had been agreed for the railway with the exception of that part of their extension which was adjacent to the Bolton railway terminus in New Bailey Street, Salford, and which was to be built by that company.

From a point just west of the station at Miles Platting the Leeds company's extension divided from the original railway to Oldham Road and ran parallel and to the north of it for some distance before passing to the north of the engine round house and descending at 1 in 49 to pass beneath Rochdale Road (formerly St. George's Road), the roadway having been raised five feet to accommodate the railway. Now falling on a gradient of 1 in 60, first on the hillside and supported by a retaining wall then, from Lower Tebbutt Street bridge, on a viaduct, the railway reached the Cheetham Hill Road bridge (formerly York Street and alternatively called Ducie Bridge). From beneath this bridge the inclination was reversed to rise at 1 in 132 into the station. This inclination, it was stated at the time, was intended to retard the trains arriving at the station to such an extent as to obviate the use of the brakes. In spite of such optimism strong buffers were provided at the end of the arrival platform. The method of dealing with arriving trains, then and for many years afterwards, was to stop them near the foot of the incline where the locomotive was detached and run into a siding, the carriages were then allowed to run by gravity into the station platform. As planned the inclination of 1 in 132 would allow departing trains to descend from the platform by gravity and without assistance to beneath the bridge where they were attached to the endless wire rope and drawn up the incline, in the event a slightly different procedure was adopted. When a train left the station the engine would draw it beneath the bridge and stop while one of the incline brake waggons was brought to the rear of the train and attached to the wire rope, communication was then made by telegraph to the engine house at the top of the incline. The wire rope was activated and the train ascended the incline, assisted partly by the incline waggon and partly by the train engine. Upon reaching the top of the incline the incline waggon was disengaged from the wire rope and the train carried on without any need to stop. Descending trains were preceded by an incline waggon immediately in front of the engine so that, if necessary, the brake could be applied and the train brought to a stand at any point on the incline. At the foot of the incline the brake waggon and the locomotive were uncoupled from the train and run forward into a

siding, the carriages were then allowed to run into the station by gravity.

As the wire rope was not operational at the time of the opening of the line it was found that two locomotives were able to haul trains of twelve carriages up the incline with ease. Indeed, less than a year later it was reported that the use of the wire rope to assist in hauling trains up the incline had all but been discontinued as locomotives were found to be quite capable of taking up the now heavier passenger and goods trains. There was, however, no doubt about the authority of the men who operated the brake waggons as was borne out by the following extract from the company rules and regulations dated August 1851:

"Bank riders have the entire control and management of the incline plane at Miles Platting, and of everything passing down; nothing to descend except conducted by them or an engine, every man upon the train implicitly following their direction."

Communication between Victoria station and Miles Platting was by means of the Cooke and Wheatstone patent electric telegraph. There were four zinc coated iron wires along the parapet of the viaduct wall and four copper wires laid underground in other places. Initially there were three uses, first for when the wire rope was required to assist a train on the incline; second, to communicate between Victoria and the engine shed when locomotives were required and third, for general communications between the station and the main line. The advantage of the electric telegraph was soon recognised to be beneficial in the working of railways, it spread rapidly throughout the country and by the end of the decade most LYR stations were placed in direct contact with the central offices at Hunts Bank. When the wires of the Electric Telegraph Company in Manchester failed in January 1849 temporary offices were provided by the LYR at Victoria station to maintain the service until repairs were completed.

Right: This small print of the west end of Victoria station shows the bridge over the river Irwell and on the right the buttress supporting the bridge over Great Ducie Street. The view of the bridge would be obliterated by an extension by the LNWR of their platform in the station and the widening of the bridge to accommodate more tracks in 1865.

The amended line of the Liverpool company was, for the majority of its length, carried on a viaduct. The junction with the Liverpool line was made to the east of Ordsall Lane from where an 'S' curve in a northerly and easterly direction brought it alongside the Bolton railway terminus at Irwell Street. Between Irwell Street and New Bailey Street the railway was carried on a viaduct designed and its erection supervised by John Hawkshaw, engineer to the Bolton company. It was supported on one side by the existing viaduct and on the south side by cast iron columns standing in pairs along the centre of Booth Street. To ensure the privacy of the inmates of the New Bailey Prison and to stifle the curiousity of the rail passengers Hawkshaw erected a screen along the south side of the viaduct, of iron plates each nine feet high by five feet wide and one inch thick. When the railway was widened in 1884 covering the remaining half of Booth Street the screen was removed. The bridge over New Bailey Street, at the east end of

the colonnade, was the subject of some concern to Salford ratepayers when it was discovered that, contrary to the Act of Parliament, the Liverpool company intended to erect a row of pillars on each side of the carriageway effectively reducing the width of the street. With the exception of four bridges the rest of the extension to Hunts Bank was carried on a brick viaduct. Three of these bridges, over Chapel Street and Gravel Lane in Salford and Great Ducie Street in Manchester, were iron arches of 83 feet in span, the rail level being about 23 feet above the carriageway. The fourth bridge, also an iron arch, carried the railway 43 feet above the river Irwell with a span of 120 feet. To enable trains from the Bolton railway access to the Manchester station a connection was provided at the west end of the New Bailey Street station, having the disadvantage that trains to Victoria were unable to call there without a reversal, it remained in use, however, until 1865 when the New Bailey Street terminus was altered to a through station.

On Friday, 3 May 1844 General Pasley inspected the railway and on Saturday, 4 May the line was opened to the general public. The Liverpool company adopted a slightly different procedure to the Leeds company when dealing with trains arriving at Victoria station. Their trains were brought to a stand by the Irwell bridge and the locomotive was run round the train which was then given a push of sufficient force to enable it to reach the arrival platform in the station.

Below: A contemporary view of the frontage of Victoria station but with the names of the two railway companies curiously transposed to show the MLR operating form the LMR side of the station and vice versa.

HEAD OFFICE +
CEMETERY EXTENSION

Prior to 1847 the administration of the Manchester and Leeds Railway was carried out at several locations in Manchester, including the Oldham Road station, a mansion at Hunts Bank and offices in the Clowes and Palatine Buildings in Hunts Bank. With the completion of Victoria station it was only natural to concentrate the headquarters of the company there. Before this could be accomplished it was decided to build an arch over the river Irk and resite Walkers Croft above it thereby giving space between the Hunts Bank Approach and Walkers Croft to erect a block of offices.

The river Irk at this period was, to quote Frederick Engels writing in 1844:

".... a narrow coal-black, foul smelling stream full of debris and refuse. .... In dry weather, a long string of the most disgusting, blackish-green slime pools are left .... from the depths of which bubbles of miasmatic gas constantly arise and give forth a stench unendurable even on the (Ducie) bridge forty or fifty feet above the surface of the stream .... (There are on the banks) heaps of debris, refuse and offal; standing pools for gutter. and a stench which alone would make it impossible for a human being in any degree civilised to live in such a district. The newly built extension of the Leeds railway, which crosses the Irk here, has swept away some of these courts and lane."

As noted earlier, the river Irk had been arched over for a distance of some thirty yards to accommodate the Hunts Bank Approach. The Leeds company now planned to cover a further ninety yards for which negotiations had been completed with the Chethams Hospital and the Grammar School who both owned the land on the southern bank. They had stipulated that the bed of the river be thoroughly cleansed out before it was covered over. Work on the culverting, which was in progress in July 1845, involved a brick span of thirty feet with a spring of eight feet six inches extending the culvert for a distance of 120 yards from the river Irwell. On the reclaimed land the Leeds company planned to build their new central offices which would include the board room and offices for the secretary, engineer and various clerks. Foundations for the building had to be excavated to a depth of between 31 and 37 feet and with the proximity of the river great care had to be taken. Though there appears to have been no official opening of the offices, the half yearly meeting of the company was held in the board room there on Wednesday, 10 March 1847. It was at this meeting that the directors suggested the future title of the company, more in keeping with the extent and importance of the united system, should be the "Lancashire and Yorkshire Railway Company". On display

in the board room was a service of silver plate weighing upwards of 3,000 ounces which had been presented to Henry Houldsworth, chairman of the Manchester and Leeds Railway Company by the directors for his services to the company.

By the early 1850s the nucleus of the Lancashire and Yorkshire Railway had been formed by amalgamations and a rapidly expanding railway network; circumstances which had a profound effect on Victoria station with its single platform. Fortunately, the pressure was alleviated to some extent by the use of Salford station for a majority of trains approaching from the west. Not a disadvantage as may at first sight be thought for it was and remained a more convenient station for the business area of Deansgate and King Street than Victoria station. In July 1844 the Bolton company had reported that few trains passed from their line over the junction to the Hunts Bank extension railway, a factor which apparently continued after the Leeds company absorbed the Bolton railway in August 1846, until December 1851. Other companies, however, sent trains to Victoria, the Preston and Wyre from April 1846 and the Lancaster and Carlisle from March 1847 advertised services to both Salford and Victoria. The Blackburn Railway and the Liverpool and Bury Railway from June and November 1848 respectively operated trains to

Salford only. Local services over the Liverpool company line had not yet been developed to a great degree but there were services and connections from the south and midlands over the Grand Junction Railway and from the north over the North Union Railway, both coming by way of Parkside, in addition to the traffic between Manchester and Liverpool.

From the opening on the 28 September 1846 the East Lancashire Railway operated trains to and from both Victoria and Salford stations until 1 May 1849 when, as a result of the Clifton Junction dispute, the company announced that all trains would arrive and depart from Salford, in addition to this the London and North Western

Railway, successors to the Liverpool and Manchester Railway, objected to the use of their railway between Salford and Victoria by the ELR. By September 1850 all LYR trains from the western division used Salford station as well. As a consequence of the continuing dispute between the LYR and the ELR over the future of the railway between Salford and Clifton Junction the terminus was the subject of a division agreement in August 1851. By the end of that year further negotiations were concluded with the result that as from the 1 January 1852 all LYR services were transferred to Victoria station giving the ELR sole use of Salford station.

To the east of Manchester the

expanding traffic came from the newly opened branch railways, Oldham in 1842 and 1847, Stalybridge in 1847, Heywood and Bury and Ardwick in 1848 and further developments in Yorkshire together with the LNWR line from Leeds and Huddersfield to Stalybridge in 1849. Earlier, it was reported that shortly after the opening of the Ashton branch in 1846, some ninety three trains per day were passing in and out of Victoria station.

To accommodate the anticipated expansion the Leeds company had, in 1846, obtained an Act of Parliament authorising the purchase of the remainder of the Walkers Croft cemetery from the Church-wardens of Manchester for

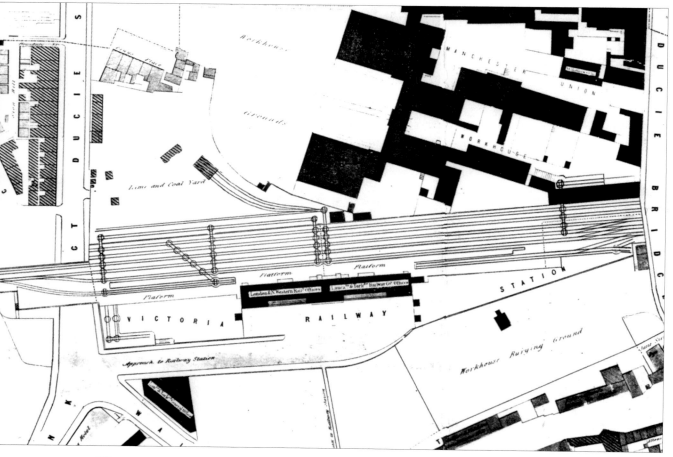

£9,874, this in addition to the £3,125 paid in 1842 for that part of the cemetery required when the Hunts Bank extension was first planned. The cemetery had been opened in 1815 and even in November 1847 interments were still taking place. Passengers to and from Victoria station were, we are told, subject to "pestilential vapours" coming from the graves which contained fifty to sixty coffins often covered with "a few boards to await the next coffin" and then covered with a minimum of earth. A decision taken in 1847 by the LYR to suspend work on new lines due to the economic situation delayed a start on the new railway until 1855 when the Parliamentary powers were about to expire.

In connection with alterations to streets at Ducie Bridge and Cheetham Hill Road, Manchester Town Council received a report from the Improvement Committee in January 1846 stating that the Leeds company engineer had

been in communication with the Council to point out that the company had plans to extend their station and that the route of the new road proposed by the Council would prevent them from doing so. As planned the new road would have been a continuation of Todd Street along Mill Brow through company land to the station and on to join Cheetham Hill Road. It was suggested that if the road were diverted leaving the area bounded by the river Irk at the disposal of the company they would be able to extend part of the station up to Long Millgate to cope with their rapidly increasing traffic. The Improvement Committee noted that the Leeds company had given notice of an application to Parliament for powers to enable them to carry out these improvements. In view of the fact that it was of sufficient public importance the committee recommended that the new road should be carried from the existing Corporation Street in a straight line to the eastern end

of Long Millgate then by a new bridge over the river Irk by Ducie Bridge to join Cheetham Hill Road. Powers were obtained by the Council in July 1853 for the purpose of extending Corporation Street involving the demolition of property and building a viaduct over the river.

The proposed extension of the station entailed the construction of a branch railway from the foot of the incline just to the east of the crossing of the river Irk to pass beneath Cheetham Hill Road and on to the land recovered from Walkers Croft cemetery. The contract for the work was awarded to Robert Neill on the 20 December 1854 for £3,365 for completion by 30 July 1855. The bridge over the river required a wrought iron tubular girder some eighty feet long by five feet deep with broad flanges top and bottom from which a number of transverse girders, four feet apart, were supported and at the other end by the existing viaduct

Left: *In the Adshead map of 1851 the station layout remained as much as it did when it was opened. The working of traffic through the station with so many turntables must have been an operator's nightmare but in spite of them there seems to have been no record of derailments or accidents due to their presence.*

Right: *In 1847 the new offices of the LYR were built to concentrate at one central and convenient location the various departments which were, hitherto, scattered in several parts of Manchester. The river Irk had been covered over and Walkers Croft built over it giving what was believed to be adequate space for the requirements of the company. However, within two decades extra space was required so the building was extended further up the Hunts Bank Approach in 1857.*

It appears that it was considered satisfactory for four inch thick timber planks to cover these girders and upon them the rails were laid. The opening beneath Cheetham Hill Road, to the south of the original bridge was carried out in two halves. Buttresses had to be erected to support the abutment of the older bridge and foundations had to be sunk forty five to fifty five feet deep. Inspite of this it was necessary to take away some of the support of the older arch and rebuild it. As is often the case in construction work of this nature there were many complaints regarding the restriction of traffic over the road and also that there was no provision made for pedestrians, women in particular experienced much difficulty making their way through the mud in wet weather. The road bridge was constructed of twelve cast iron girders with an iron plate flooring and a parapet wall of metal plates instead of brick. The bridge, which was completed before the end of l855, was wider at the south end due to alterations to the original plans made in connection with the extension of Corporation Street. A new platform was brought into use on the cemetery land towards the end of 1857. It has been difficult to establish the extent of the work but in a letter published in January 1858 a correspondent complained that the new platform ".... has for want of a shed over it been found very inconvenient in inclement weather to passengers arriving at the station". The letter was forwarded to the LYR directors who stated that the subject was under consideration.

A long wanted entrance to the station was opened from a point between the old and new bridges in Cheetham Hill Road in December 1855 when a flight of wooden stairs was erected from a point just short of the platform. Strict measures were taken to prevent the new entrance from becoming a thoroughfare between Cheetham Hill Road and Victoria Street, at first its opening was restricted to the period between 8.00am and 8.00pm. Enforcement of these directives soon prompted a complaint when a lady who had travelled to town by an omnibus from Cheetham alighted at the new entrance with the intention of meeting a friend from Yorkshire and was refused passage by the porter in charge who said that he had been given no orders to allow people to go to meet trains. She, being forced to go round to the station by Long Millgate, missed her friend. The complainant "F.T. of Cheetham Hill", husband of the lady in question, hoped that the directors having made such an improvement should make it available to all and not only to those who wished to travel by train.

The squalid approach to the station from Todd Street by way of Mill Brow remained a bone of contention for many years. A letter of the 2 November l853 describes the situation succinctly, Mill Brow ".... is exceedingly inconvenient and annoying especially in wet weather .... should you be going to the station, you descend the brow as gently as possible, arrive at the wooden bridge, and are preparing to ascend the incline plane before you, when, ten to one, down rushes a multitude, which an arrival train has just disgorged, and which, like a flood, carries all before it .... I do with all due respect (suggest) a viaduct might be built from the station to Todd Street, both being nearly on the same level". Just over two years later a meeting held on Thursday, 28 February also recommended a permanent carriageway on a viaduct. Manchester Improvement Committee reported in August 1858 that an agreement had been reached with the LYR to improve the approach to the station with the erection of a footbridge but owing to the trustees of the estate of one of the owners of an adjacent property retaining power to call for the removal of any such bridge upon six months notice, to which the Committee could not accede, the plans were postponed, much to the chagrin of pedestrians who had to continue to suffer the poor conditions of the passage aggravated by the offensive and noxius odours coming from the river for many more years.

In the day to day running of a station like Victoria there were many incidents which could be quite easily ignored but which give interesting insights. One of the correspondents, quoted above, also questioned, in 1853 the lack of a clock at the station. When the building at Hunts Bank was erected the frontage was described as having "handsome circular headed windows, with stone pilasters and dressings, and surmounted by an elegant cornice, about the centre of which is to be placed a large clock". In March 1855 it was reported that clocks were to be installed at the station one at the front of the building in the space planned and illuminated at night and another with a double dial suspended over the platform. It might be of interest to note that Greenwich Time had been adopted by the LYR in November 1847. A drinking fountain erected in 1857 on the station forecourt was destined to survive over one hundred years.

When work was being carried out on the bridge under Cheetham Hill Road an eight stall stable was built to the east of the bridge in May 1855 to accommodate the horses employed by the LYR in the passenger department and for parcels collection and delivery within the city. The LYR announced that as from the 1 January 1861 the parcels office would be transferred from the west to the east end of the station without giving a more specific location; on the same date, however, a new parcels receiving office was opened at the corner of Hunts Bank Approach and Walkers Croft in the basement of the 1847 office building.

The conditions under which people worked has been difficult to discover but occasionally some interesting aspects have come to light. Two contrasting incidents will have to suffice. On Saturday, the 15 February 1848 forty clerks employed in the Hunts Bank Offices celebrated a change in their working hours. With their working day extending from 9.00am to 7.00pm, with ninety minutes for lunch, the men found that they were unable to attend evening lectures or classes. They appealed to the LYR Board to change the hours and an agreement was reached for an eight hour day without a lunch break from 9.00am to 5.00pm. This action by the employers contrasts with some of the harsher decisions imposed on their employees in later years. The second incident ended in tragic circumstances when the station master, Thomas Reid, in attempting to prevent a man from riding on the outside of a moving train leaving the station on Saturday, 1 April 1854 was killed when he slipped and fell beneath the carriage.

The 1850s saw the introduction of horse omnibus services which operated across Manchester as distinct from the more usual habit of starting from the town centre to the outlying communities. The City Omnibus Company introduced two services in April 1852 one of which ran along Great Ducie Street to Ardwick Green giving a connection between Victoria and London Road stations. Later in the same month another service was introduced from Victoria station to Plymouth Grove. By July there were seven routes three of which made direct connection with Victoria station. In February 1862 a notice was published relating to additional omnibuses between Victoria and London Road stations, the fare being, as on previous services, 2d. These early omnibus services were the precursors of generations of public transport to and from Victoria station culminating in the most recent with the Metrolink system which opened in 1992.

Overleaf: A new innovation in 1857 was the installation of a drinking fountain on the station forecourt for the convenience of passengers. At the same time other drinking fountains were provided at London Road station and outside the Infirmary on Picadilly. Included in the rather ornate structure were drinking troughs for horses and dogs. Though its location was moved from time to time it ended its days, after more than a century of useful service, in the corner by the original station and the 1909 station building.

TOWARDS
MATURITY

SIDINGS, SHEDS + FISH MARKET

During the eighteen fifties it was becoming more obvious that alterations to the station track layout would have to be made. The situation at the west end of the station was complicated by the fact that as far as Salford station the railway was owned by the LNWR. That company was well aware of the problems and were, at meeting held in February 1858, proposing that the station be enlarged.

At the east end of the station the LYR had more of a free hand in making alterations and additions. Working the incline by the wire rope was relatively short lived for it was soon found that locomotives were able to take trains up the incline without its assistance though heavier trains required the assistance of a banking engine. By 1858 to accommodate this operation the dead end tracks inside the station, formerly reached by means of turntables, were altered to merge with the running lines beneath the Cheetham Hill Road bridge and the most northerly siding, adjacent to the workhouse retaining wall, was used as a stabling point for engines waiting to assist trains up the incline. Because of the proximity of the wall the siding, quite naturally, became known as "Wall Side" and remained so named throughout the existance of steam operation much to the curiousity of observers in later years by being as far from a wall as one could be in the station.

Confirmation of the siding for banking engines comes as a result of an accident in the station on the 9 January 1861 when it was reported that "it is customary for each train leaving for Yorkshire to be followed by a pilot engine, to assist in propelling it up the incline, and the pilot engine usually leaves the station from the opposite side (of the station) to the platform, whilst the train starts from the near side. Before the train gets under the bridge, it commences to cross the rails to the extreme left, and then the pilot engine moves forward and joins up to it". On this occasion, unfortunately, the pilot engine driver was a little too enthusiastic and ran into the side of the 3.50pm LNWR train for Leeds, derailing the engine and three of the carriages.

The change of use of these sidings in the station prevented the storage of carriages and to remedy the situation carriage sidings were provided at Newtown, about halfway up the incline; a most unlikely and unusual location. It became usual for most trains arriving at Victoria from east or west to be taken to Newtown sidings and engine drivers were instructed to be prepared to do so without the aid of a pilot engine unless absolutely necessary. Empty stock was required to leave the carriage sidings not less than twenty minutes before the train was due to leave Victoria. In 1866 an engine shed and turntable was provided to the east of the sidng to where engines could repair after bringing their carriages from the station. An incongruity of the layout of Newtown carriage sidings was the existance of a public right of way which passed beneath the main lines and between the two sets of sidings, a state of affairs which remained until the incline was widened and the sidings re-designed in 1896, though in the meantime the engine shed itself had been pulled down.

The LYR had their main locomotive depot, a round house, at Miles Platting between the Oldham Road line and the railway to Victoria. A second engine shed, a timber building, was built closer to the junction in 1843 and enlarged in 1847. A third engine shed was built opposite the round house on the south side of the Oldham Road line in 1850. These three engine sheds were replaced by Newton Heath shed in 1876.

The LNWR on the other hand had an engine shed at Ordsall Lane from the Liverpool and Manchester Railway days close to where the station would be built in 1849, it was later moved to the west side of Oldfield Road bridge and this in turn was replaced by the engine shed at Patricroft. When the extension to Victoria station was built two engine sheds were erected on the viaduct to the west of the river Irwell. By 1856 there was some concern as to the safety of these buildings for it had been

27

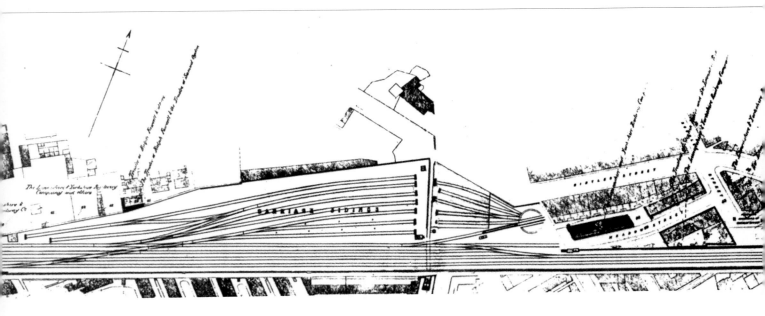

Above: Carriage sidings at Newtown were provided when it was becoming impossible to work the station and have carriages standing there. Due to the gradient it was an unusual and potentially difficult place to work so regulations were very strict. Occasionally mishaps occurred and there was at least one runaway in 1897 with fatal results. The engine shed built in the 1860s was seperated from the carriage sidings by a passage which ran under the main line. The sidings were re-organised in 1896 when the incline was widened to four tracks and the two parts were united and extended. The introduction of multiple diesel units in the 1950s diminished the need for carriages and the sidings had closed by 1973.

Left: Though it was at first intended to operate the incline to Miles Platting by means of a wire rope, it was soon found that the newer and improved locomotives were able to take trains up albeit with some assistance. The wire rope ceased to be used during the 1850s and banking engines were used for more than a century. In the restricted space at the station the most northerly siding, adjacent to the work-house wall, was used by the engines waiting to give assistance. When the station was extended in 1884 this siding could be found in the middle of the station between the old and the new parts but retained its name 'Wall Side'. This 1957 view shows a former LYR engine taking water during a lull in its days work.

discovered that the ironwork supporting the slate roof had rusted so badly that the removal of the slates was necessary. On the 23 October, however, when several men were engaged in removing the slates at the eastern end, the western end having already been attended to, the roof, for about sixty feet, collapsed and fell with a crash to the ground and also on to engines which were, at the time, being repaired.

That the LNWR had made some modifications to the track layout at the western end of Victoria station is evident from a report of an incident which occured on the 3 April 1860. It was stated that "the lines are converged upon the bridge over the Irwell, but diverged into four or five lines at the entrance to the station". At about 10.00am on the day in question, following the arrival of an LYR train from Southport, the empty carriages were being shunted to the track furthest from the platform when they collided with other carriages which were being moved to form a train to Liverpool. One of the derailed carriages ran into one of the pillars supporting the station roof, which just happened to be one of the most important in the station. A few years earlier when the fish market was opened a large opening had been made in the north wall of the station and the rails were so arranged that one of the roof pillars had to be removed and a wrought iron beam inserted between the two outer pillars, one of which was brought down together with about eighty feet of the roof. A large number of men were gathered and they were soon at work clearing the debris. One carriage was destroyed and another, a 1st class, took the whole weight of the iron beam lengthways along the roof. A massive iron bracket embedded in the masonry was prized out of its position and hung partly over Great Ducie Street and partly over the railway lines giving cause for grave concern until it was made safe. Just after 1.00pm it was possible to re-open the two central running lines through the station though in the meantime passengers arriving and departing were escorted to trains which were stopped on the river bridge. There were many comments about the accident mainly to the effect that the opportunity should be taken to build a completely new station.

Reference made above to the fish market requires some elaboration. In 1856 negotiations had taken place between the LYR and Manchester Corporation Markets Committee regarding the supplies of fish from the Yorkshire coastal fishing ports and the inadequate market facilities in Manchester. The LYR offered to provide facilities on their land at the corner of Great Ducie Street and New Bridge Street on a twenty one year lease at a rental of £230 per annum. The accommodation consisted of a series of arches extending from the north wall of the train shed upon which a siding was laid through the wall. Facilities were provided to allow baskets or barrels of fish to be lowered to the market floor below and the arches to be used by the traders for various purposes. Offices and display facilities were also provided all being roofed over. A gated vehicular access fronted directly on to Great Ducie Street. The new market, which was opened in June 1856, was a distinct improvement but as will be seen later was to be a short lived venture. It may come as a surprise the amount of trouble taken by the LYR but fish traffic had become an important aspect of the station work for, in the herring season alone at this period, there could be as many as sixteen wagons arriving daily each carrying twenty barrels with $2^1/_2$ to 3cwt. of fish in each barrel.

STATION EXTENSIONS
+ SALFORD LINE

By the eighteen sixties the capacity of the double track railway between Victoria station and Salford was almost certainly stretched to the very limit. Similarly, the station itself must have become a nightmare for the operating staff and completely inadequate to deal with the amount of traffic.

Criticism was mounting both from within the company and from the public at large. A shareholder had complained at the half yearly meeting in February 1859 of the lack of waiting rooms and another person wrote in the October about the "lack of facilities for finding trains .... and a general defectiveness as to direction of the few available porters .... At the seasons of pressure there is an amount of inconvenience and danger resulting from the plan of the station and its management". Four months later it was stated that "Scenes might, a short time ago at least, be witnessed there in the third class ticket office, through the total inadequacy of the space, aggravated doubtless by the stupid pracitise issuing the tickets only five minutes before the starting of the train, which beggared description. On an ordinary Saturday night it was absolutely dangerous for women or children to attempt to get a ticket and the smallest danger incurred was that of the loss of articles of dress in the crush and scuffle". One person writing in March 1860 referred to "the railway porters at Victoria station whose conduct to third class passengers is notoriously rude .... but being equal to any of these .... I have been able to make them know their true position".

In November 1860 the LYR applied for powers to build a new railway on a viaduct adjacent to and north of the existing viaduct from Salford station to Victoria and to enlarge that station. Opposition to the Bill came from the LNWR who, whilst agreeing that it was necessary to make improvements, felt that what was needed was the enlargement and entire reconstruction of Victoria station itself. Salford town council also opposed the Bill but readily withdrew when offered compensation to the value of £25,000 to be spent on improvements in the borough, one of which was the erection of a new road bridge over the river Irwell being an extension of Chapel Street to Victoria Street on the Manchester side almost opposite Hunts Bank Approach and completed in August 1864.

The powers for the new railway and extension of the station were granted in June 1861. The LNWR agreed to continue to honour an agreement to allow the LYR traffic to pass over the viaduct between Salford and Victoria station and through the LNWR portion of that station to the LYR property until the L&Y had completed their own viaduct but not to exceed beyond five years from the 1 August 1861.

At the east end of the station improvements included the replacement of the Cheetham Hill Road bridge with one of iron giving a span of 135 feet and supported by iron columns. The work entailed the closure of the road for about four months, the new bridge being opened on Saturday, 2 September 1865. Along Walkers Croft from the new bridge to the footbridge over the river Irk at Mill Brow a massive retaining wall was erected enclosing what was left of the Walkers Croft cemetery. The unearthing of coffins and human remains prompted cries of indignation, for it was reported that the coffins were broken open by the workmen and the remains wheeled in barrows a distance of twenty yards before being tipped beside the wall. To the present day it is not unusual for bones to be unearthed at the station when excavations are taking place.

Upon the reclaimed land a new extension of the station was built which included four platform faces of about 450 feet long and on one was erected a block of waiting rooms and other facilities 168 feet long and narrowing somewhat from 30 feet wide. Across the platform ends a new two storey stone building was erected housing a booking office and other administrative offices.

To accomodate the new station roof the workhouse retaining wall was raised twelve feet, the roof now extending in three spans to Walkers Croft

Above: + right: A rare but unfortunately poor view of the 1865 booking office at the turn of the century and shortly before the construction of the bay platform extensions. To the right can be seen the roof over the earlier bay platform, part of which is still standing 140 years later. A cab horse is taking a welcome drink from the fountain. In 1905 the same building was decorated for the visit of the King and Queen who came to Manchester to formally open the new No. 9 dock at the Ship Canal. Very soon this booking office would be demolished to make way for the restaurant and grill room as part of the station extension.

National Railway Museum

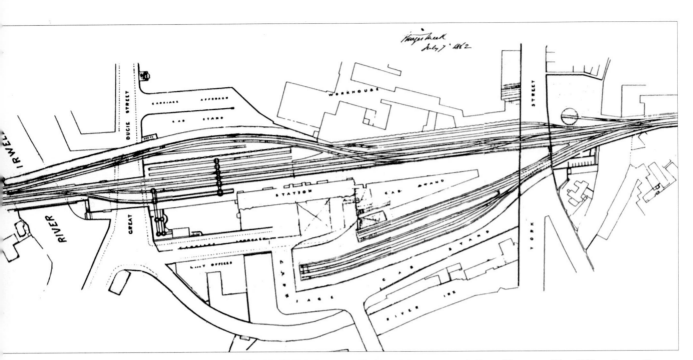

Above: The LYR engineer Sturges Meek provided this diagram in July 1862 to show his plan for the extension of the station. The plan included four new bay platforms for local traffic to the east of Manchester but no alterations to the through lines due to opposition by the LNWR to the proposals. The only change proposed at the west end was the construction of a new LYR line from Salford that cut through the north wall of the train shed and included a new east bound platform. He envisaged a reversed inclined carriageway for vehicles from Great Ducie Street up to the new platform and on the south side there would be a bridge over the river Irk from Long Millgate. In the event not all of the plan materialised.

Left: When the LYR applied for powers to build their new railway from Salford to Victoria station they were opposed vehemently by Salford Corporation and clauses were inserted into the final Act that resulted in the LYR paying over £25,000 in acknowledgement of the damage done to the borough. The money had to be spent on improvements on the north side of Chapel Street. In the event, it was decided to build a bridge over the river Irwell opposite the Palatine Hotel being a continuation of Chapel Street. When the bridge was opened on the 24 August 1864 it was reported to have cost £20,000; it was rebuilt in 1912.

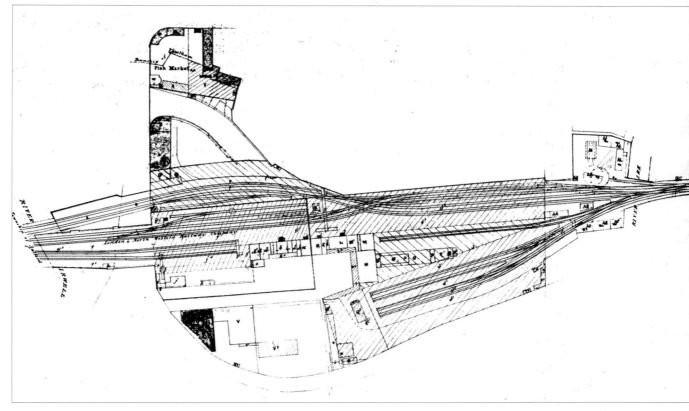

and from Great Ducie Street to Cheetham Hill Road bridge.

At the west end the LNWR extended their part of the main platform and built a new bay platform 300 feet long in the process widening the bridge over Great Ducie Street with flat girders on the south side but before the work was completed a further extension to the west side of the river Irwell was decided upon together with new roofing over both platforms. In addition, the offices formerly used by the LNWR station master and other officials were converted into commodious and well appointed waiting rooms and a roof was erected over the cab stand, the officials being found alternative accommodation.

The major part of the LYR improvements at the west end was the erection of the brick viaduct from Salford station, which was converted from a terminus to a through station, to Victoria where bridges were built over the river Irwell and Great Ducie Street. The new line passed outside the train shed at the LNWR end of the station and through an opening in the north wall into the LYR half of the station. A new platform, 670 feet long, was placed on the east bound track from the river bridge to the workhouse wall. In the process the fish market was re-sited closer to New Bridge Street with the loss of direct rail access. A new station approach was provided from Great Ducie Street together with a flight of stairs up the side of the viaduct to the east bound platform above. A footbridge was erected from the new platform to the old opposite the centre of the

Above: Apart from one important point this unidentified plan of about 1866 shows the layout of the station as it would remain for the next twenty years. In this plan the LNWR lines through the LYR side of the station are shown to join the two northerly tracks whereas in fact they joined the second and third tracks leaving the most northerly track (Wall Side) for the use of banking engines. Another change was the removal of the turntable and engine shed in the north east corner to Newtown carriage sidings. Note also that the fish market has been re-located in the corner of Great Ducie Street and New Bridge Street where it would remain until 1873 when the business was transferred to the new fish market at Shudehill. Another change shown was the extension of the company offices further up Hunts Bank Approach.

original station building and all platforms in the station were raised to what was regarded as the 'normal height.' A problem which soon arose was the habit of some passengers to cross the rails instead of using the footbridge. Because the older platform was higher and the newer one had a ramp down to rail level it was often that offenders went from the old to the new platform unless apprehended by station staff and threatened with a summons. The LYR platform inside the station was widened by the simple expedient of covering the original platform road. There were now four tracks through the L&Y side of the station, the northerly line or 'wall side' used by banking engines, two through roads used by both the L&Y and the LNWR and the platform road which curved sharply across the LNWR lines in the centre of the station to gain access to the new lines to Salford. The LNWR continued to use the original platform in their part of the station, not widened but extended, for passenger trains in both directions.

In July 1865 the new railway and station extensions were inspected by a Board of Trade official and were opened to the public on Tuesday, 1 August.

At about the same time as the station extensions were taking place the LYR and LNWR agreed to the addition of a second storey above the central section of the original Hunts Bank station building.

In May 1866 a suggestion was made that to avoid the confusion that regularly occurred at the station all the platforms be numbered, lettered or even named because, it was

said, the travelling public often found that the calls of the porters were unintelligible.

As noted above, the fish market had to be moved to accommodate the new extensions which resulted in the fish traffic being transported by road from Oldfield Road, Salford, a distinctly unsatisfactory arrangement creating considerable conjestion in Great Ducie Street. The problem was finally resolved when the Corporation built a completely new wholesale and retail market adjacent to the Smithfield fruit and vegetable market in Shudehill and that at Great Ducie Street was closed on the 14 February 1873.

Following the success of the patent brake invented in 1857 by Charles Fay, the LYR carriage superintendent, passenger trains were able to descend the incline to Victoria without the precautionary assistance of the break wagons stationed at Miles Platting. With the advantage of the break almost all local passenger trains descending the incline came to a halt or almost before the junction to the bay platforms, the guard disconnnecting the coupling between the carriages and the engine by means of a device in his van, the engine then ran forward, and the carriages now under the control of the guard ran into one of the bay platforms.

Apart from the adherence of the time interval system to restrict trains from following each other with less than five minutes between them there was little or no control of trains up or down the incline except by signals spaced about 100 yards apart until 1865 when a form of

electric telegraph was introduced by which information was conveyed to Victoria giving notice of the type of train to expect but not the number of trains. Reliance depended on the time interval system being adhered to, which was not always the case. On the 16 July 1866 the block telegraph was first introduced through five signal cabins, No.5 being at Victoria station opposite the junction of the lines into the bay platforms. This system was improved by the introduction, a few years later of the absolute block system using Tyers block instruments and interlocked lever frames. The numbering of the signal cabins was at this time reversed with No.1 being at Victoria station and No.5 at the top of the incline a short distance before Miles Platting station.

Right: *Once plans had been agreed for the extension of the station the erection of the new buildings could begin. Retaining the whole of the original station building a new booking office was built at right angles to the old, facing down Hunts Bank Approach. New bay platforms were provided on the south side with an overall roof, part of which survives to the present day with columns embossed with the date and the builder's name. Though the main parcel office was within the main station a receiving and collection office was opened in the basement of the 1847 office building in 1861. There are several 'ghosts' about the forecourt due to the long shutter exposures required by the plate cameras of the day. Apart from the Hunts Bank Approach there was a footway leading from the forecourt to Long Millgate and Corporation Street. This would be improved by the next station extension in 1884 but completely replaced twenty years later. The new twentieth century office block was built between the central raised part of the 1844 building and the booking office of 1865 which of course was then demolished.*

WORKHOUSE ACQUISITION +
PLATFORM DEVELOPMENTS

Before the completion of the works of the 1865 extension a small parcel of land was required which belonged to the Manchester Board of Guardians and for which the LYR had made an offer of £165 upon the understanding that the Guardians were at liberty to build on the foundations of the wall and use the land behind it. The company were at pains to point out that the work would not only improve the appearance of the boundary wall between the two properties but would enable them to ease the curves of the new line into the station. The Guardians, at a meeting held on the 6 October 1865 rejected the overtures but they did report that they would consider any proposition from the LYR to purchase the whole of the workhouse property. Further reports in July 1866 and June 1867 revealed that extensions and replacements to the workhouse were necessary but in consequence of the activities of the LYR any expenditure would be inadvisable in view of the possibility of the railway company taking the workhouse premises. In May 1872 the Board of Guardians were informed that Thomas Dugdale, chairman of the LYR had been authorised to negotiate with the Guardians for the purchase of the premises and by September it was reported that an agreement had been reached for the sale of the property, comprising 18,618 square yards, for

£95,000, to be paid in installments, the first of which was £20,000. The Guardians retained a portion of the property, including offices and some other buildings covering an area of 5,608 square yards. Before the property could be released to the LYR, however, it was necessary to build a replacement infirmary. Although the indenture of the conveyance was signed and sealed in February 1874 this was deleted and it was not until July 1881 that the transfer was formally finalised. In 1854 the Board of Guardians had purchased an estate in Crumpsall, north of Manchester, upon which to build a new workhouse owing to the overcrowded conditions at New Bridge Street so it was decided to build the new infirmary at the same place. Even after the infirmary foundation stone had been ceremoniously laid in November 1876 the weather and a long strike of joiners and carpenters contributed to delay completion. Meanwhile the LYR who had been promised access to at least a portion of the New Bridge Street property, were frustrated beyond measure. At last, following the completion of some new buildings at the New Bridge Street offices in September 1880, it was possible to give up to the LYR so much of the land that they would require immediately for the extension of Victoria station.

Although the new works of

1865 had more than doubled the size of the station less than ten years later there was pressure for further extensions. Following an accident in October 1872 a Board of Trade inspector reported that "a one sided station, which necessarily converts a double line into a single line, at a place where trains meet from various directions, must always be dangerous. It is to be hoped that the LYR and the LNWR companies will take the first opportunity to improve Victoria station. The station, as now divided and apportioned between the two companies, is bad and dangerous. If re-arranged and worked as a joint station, it could be very much improved. There is very good access to the station from both sides at present".

One of the most serious obstacles was the double track Hunts Bank incline and the bottleneck of Miles Platting station; indeed it was stated at a meeting held in February 1873, that it was becoming impossible to work traffic through that station and it was proposed that a loop from the proposed Prestwich line to Newton Heath was essential and also the widening of the railway from Victoria to Newton Heath. Powers for a railway from Victoria to Radcliffe and Bradley Fold, through Cheetham Hill and Prestwich had been obtained in July 1872. In June 1873 an Act authorised the loop from Cheetham Hill to the main line at Newton Heath, this stretch of railway subsequently became known as the Manchester Loop Line. In the event the widening of the incline was not proceeded with at this time and another proposed line, a spur from the Manchester Loop tunnelling beneath Miles Platting station to make a connection with the Ashtom branch was withdrawn from a Bill before Parliament in 1876. The Acts of 1872 and 1873 also authorised the construction of a new railway from Newton Heath through Failsworth and Hollinwood to join the Oldham branch railway at Werneth avoiding the notorious 1 in 27 incline between Middleton Junction and Oldham. In November 1877 the LYR gave notice of an application for

Below: Following approaches to the Board of Guardians agreement was finally reached for the purchase of a major portion of the workhouse property. The layout of that part of the station to the north of the original platform is shown after the extension of 1865 with the LYR line cutting sharply across the LNWR line in the centre of the station, past the eastbound platform and on towards Salford station. When the bridge under Cheetham Hill Road, here given the old name of York Street, was completed work was started, after much delay, to clear the site within the heavy line and the construction of the new extension in 1884.

Overleaf: By the turn of the century there were only two major extensions to be attended to. The first, shortly after the date of this map, 1889, was the provision of two additional tracks on the incline to Miles Platting, completed in 1896, and the second was the erection of an entirely new suburban station with ten platforms extending southwards to Long Millgate together with the block of offices. One confusing aspect of the station was the use of a single number for two platform faces, as on platforms 2, 6, 7 and 8, similarly in Exchange station platform 2 applied to two platform faces. One of the most serious disadvantages at Exchange station was the fact that the only way for vehicles to gain access to the road-way between platforms 3 and 4 (later re-numbered 4 and 5) was by passing from the station forecourt down an incline, beneath part of the station and then climbing another incline to the platform level. This was remedied when a new bridge from Hunts Bank was joined to the Chapel Street bridge giving easier access without having to go up the old station approach. It should be noted that Hunts Bank from the Cathedral to Great Ducie Street had not yet been re-named Victoria Street.

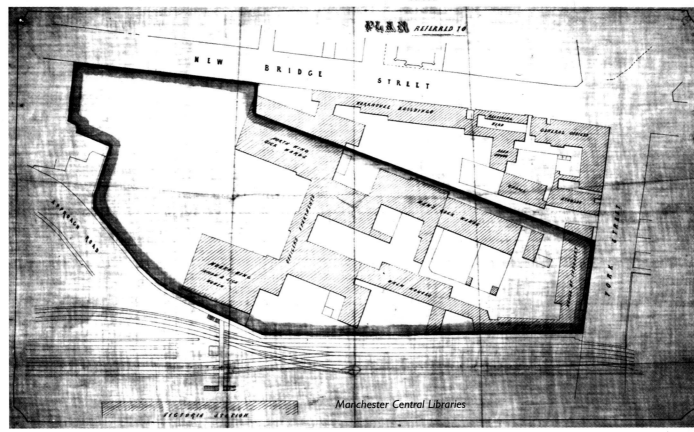

Manchester Central Libraries

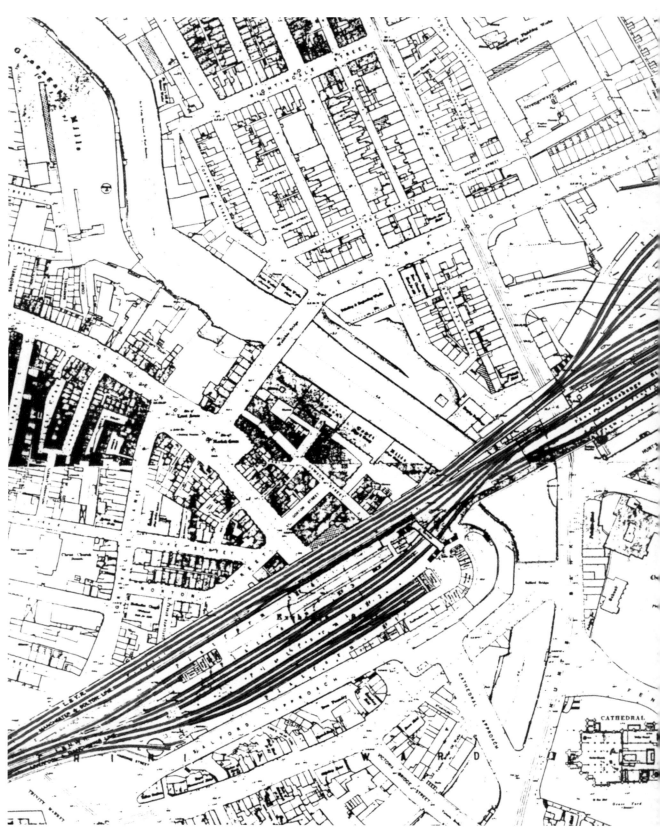

powers for a short length of railway from the east side of Great Ducie Street to a point on the Manchester Loop, about fifty yards east of the junction with the incline, which would pass through the workhouse property and require either a new opening beneath Cheetham Hill Road or a new bridge entirely.

It can be seen that crucial to all the planning was the acquisition of the workhouse property which, as has been related, was not forthcoming, at least, not at the time which the LYR had anticipated. The delay had left the company in a difficult position for the contract for the Loop line which had been let to Taylor and Thomson for £107,194 in March 1874 was expected to be completed by the summer of 1877 though it was not until February 1878 that it was reported that goods traffic was using the new railway. Following several postponements the Board of Trade inspector authorised the opening for passenger traffic which took place on Thursday, 1 August 1878. The Loop line was planned for four tracks throughout, the southern pair being the slow lines which branched from the main line at Victoria East Junction.

The Prestwich line which branched off the Loop line at Cheetham Hill Junction, just under a mile from Victoria, had taken several years to complete, mainly because of delays in the purchase of land, the contract was not awarded to Thomas Waller until February 1876 but on Monday, 1 September 1879 it was possible to open the first section of the railway from Cheetham Hill to Whitefield for

passenger traffic and to Radcliffe on the 1 December. On that day the train service between Manchester and Bacup, which hitherto ran from Radcliffe through Clifton Junction and Salford to Manchester was re-routed over the new line. At Victoria, because of the difficutlies experienced in obtaining the workhouse land, a temporary terminus was built on what would later be the site of the railway into the station, just to the east of Cheetham Hill Road bridge The contract for the terminus, Ducie Bridge as it would be called, was let in April 1879 and the station was ready to be used by special trains on the occasion of a Grand Review and Sham Fight which took place in Heaton Park on Saturday, 30 August just two day before the public opening of the Prestwich line.

The method of working Ducie Bridge station, which consisted of a single island platform with one line on either side entered from the slow line of the Manchester Loop, the fast line not having been laid at this time, gave some cause for concern especially after an accident there in 1883. It seems that, because of the shortness of the platforms, more than twenty of the thirty six trains which arrived there could not be accommodated with the engine. So, as the trains approached, it was customary for the engine to be detached whilst the train was still in motion and run forward beyond the points which were rapidly changed and the carriages then ran into the platform under the control of the guard. Though this practise

was in complete variance with the rule book it had been found that if a train was brought to a stand and the engine detached in the correct manner it was difficult, or impossible, to restart the train by gravity. Fortunately, because of the temporary nature of the operation the company was allowed to continue the practise.

As an aside, it is interesting that the Ducie Bridge station was described as being at the foot of Jacobs Ladder. Jacobs Ladder was, in fact, a series of flights of stairs which descended from Cheetham Hill Road to Vernon Street adjacent to the river Irk just before the river plunged beneath the railway. Generations of railway enthusiasts have watched train movements from these steps at the east end of Victoria station, up the incline and towards Red Bank until British Railways erected a monstrosity of a power signal box in 1962 which effectively obliterate the view.

In September 1880 the LYR was in a position to start the reconstruction of the Cheetham Hill Road bridge and though the work was considerably advanced by October 1881 it was reported in May 1882 that the Town Clerk had been advancing methods for the quicker expedition of the work and William Hunt, the LYR engineer stated that it was not possible to engage more workmen as there was no space for them to work and that the contractors had been, for a period, working both day and night.

With the completion of the bridge it was possible to open the horse tram car service between Albert Square and

Cheetham Hill on Thursday, 27 July 1882 when the first car passed over the bridge at 7.45am.

Work on the station extension entailed the erection of a new retaining wall to support the remaining part of the workhouse property and the excavation of the intervening earth which was to be tipped on land reclaimed by the diversion of the river Irk about half a mile along the Manchester Loop from Victoria. It was reported in December 1881 that the earth moving would start as soon as the company had completed the necessary rail connection and signal installations. Because the old station roof had been supported by the workhouse wall it was necessary to provide adequate support in the form of iron columns before the wall could be removed. The portion of the old wall in the LNWR half of the station would remain for many years and was often

shown in the background of photographs at the west end of platform twelve.

Once started, the work proceeded with alacrity so much so that it was possible to bring the first part of the extension into use on Monday, 31 March 1884. On the preceding Saturday, Ducie Bridge station was closed and on the following day all trains arrived and departed at the bay platforms, on Monday platform seven was brought into use. It was then possible to remove the east-bound platform of the 1865 extension together with the footbridge which connected it with the main part of the station. By Thursday, 1 May, the new platforms six and eight were completed and brought into use. The new extension now consisted of two island platforms over 800 foot long, number six (later re-numbered twelve and thirteen), number seven (fourteen and fifteen) and

a single platform with a bay at the east end number eight (sixteen and seventeen). Trains for Rochdale and the Yorkshire district and also traffic for Preston, the Fylde coast and Scotland were designated to use platform six, platform seven was to be used by trains to the East Lancashire area and platform eight catered for arrivals at the station from the west and the Prestwich branch trains in the bay from the east. Platform five in the older side of the station continued to deal with trains for Liverpool, Southport and west Lancashire together with arrivals from the Yorkshire area.

On each of the island platforms booking offices, waiting rooms and other facilities were provided; platform eight had waiting rooms but no booking office. A subway, twenty four feet wide, connected the "Blackpool departure platform", number

Right and following drawings: *Erected to the west of the subway across the station the booking office stood on platform 6 (later 12 and 13). There were seven ticket windows to serve the LYR and one for the Midland railway. At the rear right hand side was the inspector's office and on the opposite side was the Midland Railway booking office which was closed in 1913 when the station was 'closed'. Stairs at the rear of the building gave access to the station master's office which occupied the whole of the upper floor and from which an overall view of the station could be obtained. A clock was provided on all four sides of the building. Following the blitz in 1940 all ticket booking was concentrated at the main booking office on Victoria Station Approach. The platform booking office building was finally demolished in 1992.*

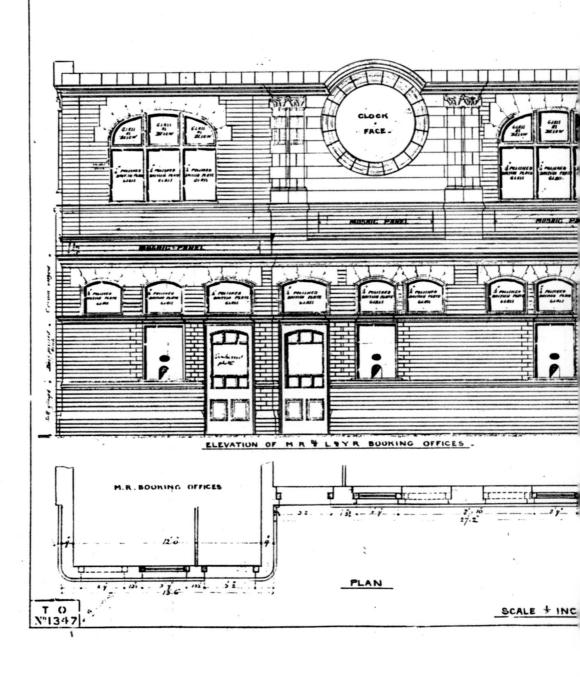

ELEVATION OF M R & L & Y R BOOKING OFFICES.

PLAN

VICTORIA STATION 2339 N° 6.

ECRAPH OFFICE &c ON N°6 PLATFORM

WINDOW TO INSPECTORS ROOM &c.

PLAN.

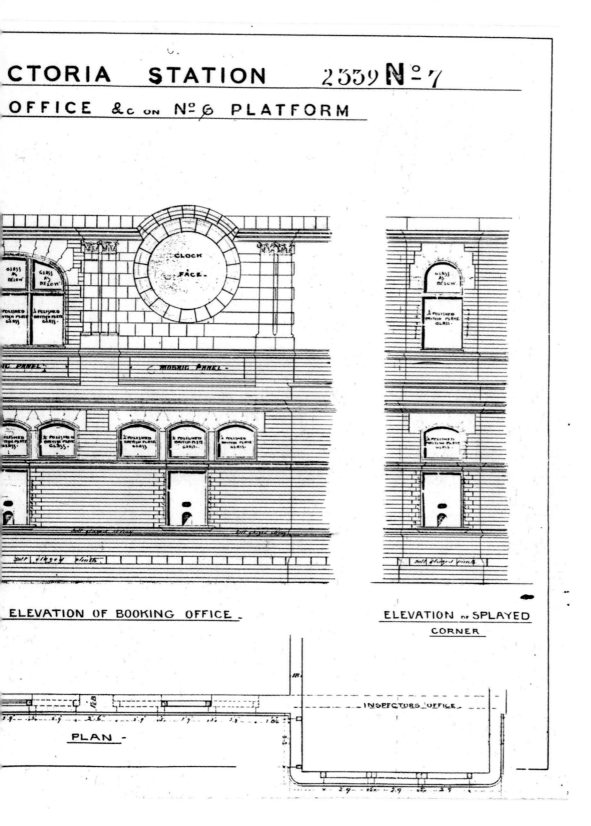

CTORIA STATION 2359 N° 7

OFFICE &c ON N° 6 PLATFORM

ELEVATION OF BOOKING OFFICE.

ELEVATION OF SPLAYED CORNER

PLAN.

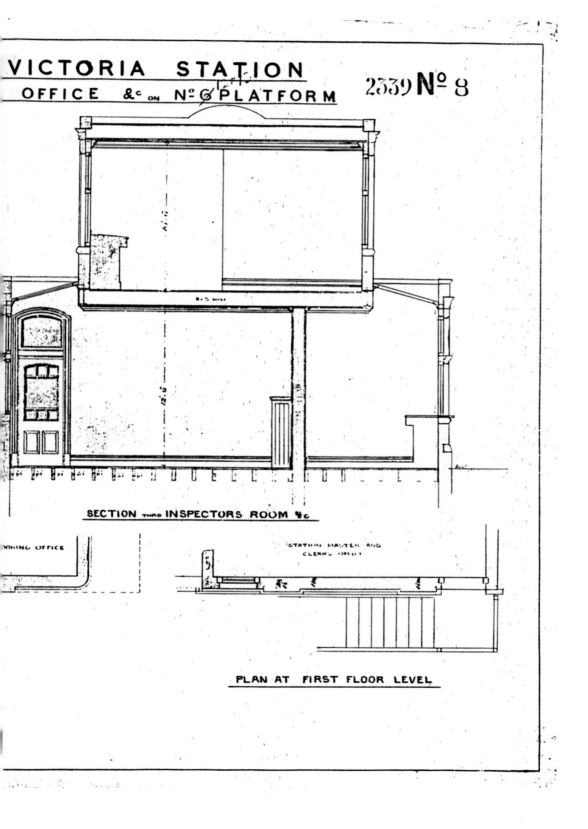

VICTORIA STATION
OFFICE &c ON Nº 6 PLATFORM   2339 Nº 8

SECTION THRO INSPECTORS ROOM &c

PLAN AT FIRST FLOOR LEVEL

National Railway Museum

National Railway Museum

Left: When the new station extension was opened in 1884 the vehicular approach from Great Ducie Street passed beneath the railway to platform 6 (later 12 and 13) rising up by an incline to the platform level immediately in front of the booking office. However, when it was decided to 'close' the platforms off and institute ticket barriers the incline was closed in 1912 and luggage lifts provided and railings erected around the booking office. The only way onto the platforms was by having a valid ticket or a platform ticket obtained from a dedicated machine near the barriers.

In the upper view the new arrangements can be recognised also the track of the overhead parcels carrier in the roof girders and a couple of engines patiently waiting at the far end of Wall Side. The luggage bridge had been built when this part of the station was built giving access to each platform and the subway and was extended when the suburban station was built. The overhead parcel carrier, erected in 1895, complemented the luggage bridge giving quick access to all the platforms in the station.

In the lower view the station roof stops just short of the platform ends which were protected by short canopies. The whole of this part of the station was destroyed in the blitz` of 1940. When the debris was removed the platforms remained open to the elements until December 1992 when the site was cleared to make way for the new stadium complex which was opened in July 1995.

five, with the new platforms, there were stairs up to platform six and inclined passages to five, seven and eight. The subway was divided lengthwise into two, the west side for passengers and the east side for conveying luggage and parcels and for this purpose four hydraulic hoists were installed for transferring luggage between the subway and the platforms. An entrance to platform eight opened directly from New Bridge Street and a road approach from Great Ducie Street passed beneath part of the extension and up an incline to the booking office on platform six. There was space for between twenty and thirty cabs on this incline, a cabmens shelter was provided on one side and an excursion booking office on the other. In the early twentieth century this incline was removed and replaced by two flights of stairs and two hoists, the platform being extended over the resulting space. Also from the Great Ducie Street approach were two inclined passages, one leading to platform seven and the other to platform eight. The stairs which formerly ascended from Great Ducie Street to the old 1865 platform were retained but realigned to serve platform eight.

On the north side of the extension the station roof was supported partly by the workhouse retaining wall and partly by a new wall along New Bridge Street. The main part of the roof was supported by a series of iron columns running across at right angles to the new platforms. There were ten bays topped by semi-circular arched girders which supported the glazed roof and ventilation appertures. From the east to the west the main roof was just over 200 yards long though the platforms at the west end which poked out from under its mantle had individual coverings. For reasons which are not clear, a roof was erected over the bridge carrying the railway over Great Ducie Street into the new extension, this roof had been installed when the bridge was built in 1865 and was reconstructed in 1885 following its re-alignment and slight widening in 1884. At the general meeting in February 1885 it was reported, with some alarm, that the station extension had required additional staff which would cost nearly £2,000 per annum.

Giving evidence before a committee of inquiry in 1875 the station master, John Jackson, reported that he had five signal cabins under his jurisdiction and fourteen signalmen at Victoria station. After the implementation of the block system on the LYR in 1869 four cabins were worked by three men working eight hour shifts and the fifth by two men working twelve hour shifts each of the latter being relieved one day a week. Prior to the introduction of the eight hour shift system it was not unusual for a signalman to be required to work extra hours over his normal twelve hour shift. In addition there were several relief signalmen under a superintendent who could be called upon when a regular signalman was ill or otherwise indisposed. Each of the signal cabins at the station were visited daily by the station master or one of his inspectors and at night by a travelling inspector.

Further improved signalling, a consequence of the extension of the station took the form of four signal cabins connected by telephone, one at the west end of platform five in the junction with the LNWR lines and the other on the north side of the railway to the east of Great Ducie Street bridge. At the east end of the station two cabins were adjacent to the east side of the Cheetham Hill Road bridge, one at the end of platform five to deal with the bay platform traffic and the other on the north side of the railway, these two signal cabins were shortly to be replaced, in 1889, by Victoria East Junction signal cabin. There was a supplementary office between these two signal cabins used by the inspectors who controlled the arrangement and working of trains in and out of the station. One highly dangerous movement which was done away with at this time and which dated back to the opening of the station in 1844, was the practise of detaching the locomotives from trains arriving at the east end of the station and then allowing the carriages to descend by gravity into a platform. The new method adopted was for the train to run into the station, unload the passengers then either another engine would take the train out or the original train engine would set the carriages back out of the platform, then run into a siding and allow the carriages to roll into an appropriate platform. This system was used until the end of locomotive hauled passenger trains.

Contrary to later practise it seems that the south face of platform six (12) was used for eastbound trains as had the 1865 platform which it replaced. At east junction trains leaving this platform could travel up the incline or along the loop line. Trains using the other platforms in the new extension could only gain access to the fast line on the loop and vice versa, west bound trains from the incline and loop slow line could only use the through lines or platform five (11). To remedy this apparent incongruity the north side of the incline was widened to the east of the junction in about 1890 and a short double track spur

was laid across the loop slow line and then immediately merged with the up and down lines on the incline thus making it possible for trains to and from the incline to use any platform in the station. A legacy of the use of platform six (12) by eastbound trains was recorded by Eric Mason in his description of the working of Victoria station in the early years of the twentieth century when he stated that there were three eastbound trains using that platform. By the period which he was describing this platform was used predominately by

westbound trains to the Fylde coast, eastbound trains mostly used platform thirteen.

In connection with the new extension of the station the old and disreputable approach from Todd Street by way of Mill Brow and the footbridge over the river Irk was done away with and a new, level roadway, Victoria Station Approach, was built in 1884, together with a row of shops along the east side, from Long Millgate towards the station in 1886.

Co-incidentally with the station extensions work was proceeding on the enlargement

Left upper: *The Great Ducie Street entrance to the 1884 station extension was flanked on one side by the new parcel office built in 1894. The building also accommodated the Passenger Traffic Superintendent department on the first floor and later, in 1915, the Central Control Office on the top floor. As built in 1884 there were entrances to all three platforms until the station was 'closed' in 1913 when passengers had to use the subway from the main part of the station with the exception of contract holders.*

Left lower: *Very few photographs appear to have been taken of the New Bridge Street side of Victoria station. This one shows the entrance to the mainline platforms but also includes the austere and forbidding presence of the workhouse property extending onwards to Cheetham Hill Road. Sometimes referred to as the Bastille the workhouse frequently struck terror into some of the more unfortunate townsfolk.*

Opposite right: *Within a few years space in the office building at the junction of Hunts Bank Approach and Walkers Croft became restricted and so it was extended further up towards the station in 1857 and again in 1884 along Victoria Station Approach as far as the river Irk with flights of steps up from Walkers Croft. The accompanying floor plans (overleaf) easily illustrates the development of the office complex from the first building through the intermediate extension of 1857 to the final 1884 extension. Vacated in 1970, the buildings were seriously damaged by fire in 1975 and then demolished in 1978 with the site area landscaped.*

of the Hunts Bank headquarters building. The first office block had been built in 1847 at the corner of Walkers Croft and to this an extension was added further up Hunts Bank Approach in 1857. By the 1880s it was obvious that there was a need for much larger office accommodation and it was decided to extend the building, to the top of Hunts Bank and along Victoria Station Approach as far as the river Irk. The tender of Robert Neill, £27,242, was recommended to be accepted on the 8 April 1884 for this building which had four floors and, because of difference in floor levels, there were steps up from the corridor in the older building. At the south end between the second and third floors an intermediate floor was inserted. The erection of the building was not without incident for on Wednesday, 8 October, 1884 a steam crane lifting a stone landing into position failed causing serious injuries to two men who were struck by the falling stonework. Although there seems to have been no official opening the half yearly meeting on Wednesday,

10 February, 1886 was held in the new offices.

The station master, J.H.Sedgwick, had his office on the floor above the booking office on platform six. Sedgwick, who had been appointed station master in 1879, remained in office until his retirement in October 1911; he died very shortly afterwards on the 20 January, 1912. A previous station master, John Jackson, who had served at Victoria station for twenty two years, though not necessarily as station master during all that time, and who had retired in January 1876 also failed to survive more than three months, for he was found dead having committed suicide in his public house on the 14 March, 1876. For people who had the misfortune to die at the station, such as an LNWR employee who was killed in December 1875, the bodies were taken to the LYR "dead house" to await an inquest, though just where in the station this mortuary was situated was not revealed.

Both companies made some attempts to encourage the spirtiual, mental and physical

well being of their employees at the station. Religious services were arranged to be held once a week and as early as 1854 libraries were established at several L&Y stations, that at Victoria was to share a donation of £100 given by the directors towards this end; indeed even in 1930, and probably much later, books were being issued from the library at the station which still displayed the LYR rules and date stamp inside the cover. Inter-departmental competitive sports meetings were frequently arranged, one such was a cricket match between two elevens from the audit office on the 4 July 1868 when the passenger section defeated the goods section by 38 runs.

Though the new extensions to the station were a precursor to the rejuvenation of the LYR some old habits and opinions took longer to fade away; one such was the reputation of the company for the late running of trains which prompted the following incident in 1885:

"A Middleton mother took her two growing lads to Manchester one Saturday with half tickets. Full fare was demanded by the

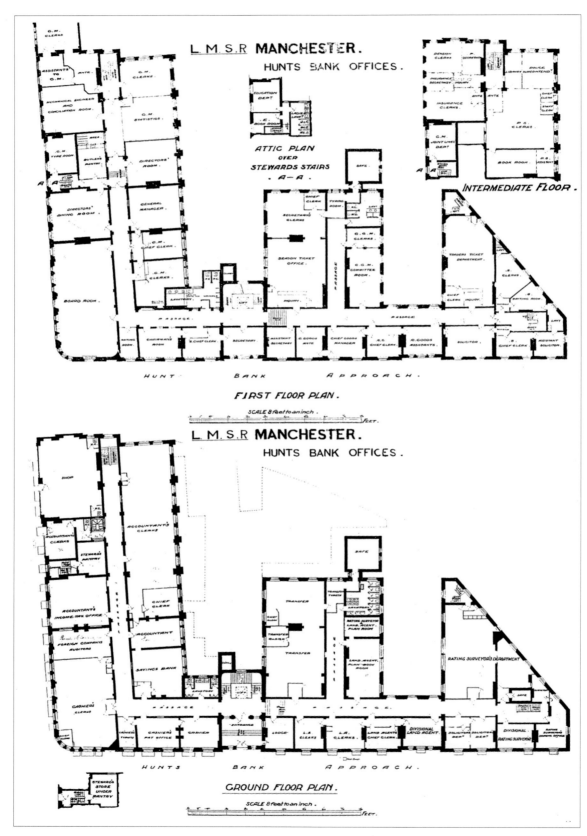

city collector who insisted that the boys were 'full age long ago'. 'Ieigh', replied the irate mater, 'May be they are neaw but they weren't when wi' left Middleton."

Left: *This 1930s LMSR plan of the Hunts Bank offices illustrates the development from the triangular 1847 building to the central block extension of 1857 to the final extension along Victoria Station Approach in 1885.*

Right: *"The success of the library surpasses the most sanguine expectations of the promoters" so it was reported a year after the Manchester Free Library had been opened in September 1852. Of the 4,857 readers in the first year many were still queueing when the library was about to close each evening at 9.00pm. Quite possibly stimulated by this success John Dunston, the young secretary of the LYR, persuaded the directors that there was a similar demand from their employees. The Board saw fit to make a donation of £100 towards the establishment of libraries at certain stations, providing rooms for its furtherance. On their part the railway men organised fund raising events the proceed going towards improving facilities. In July 1855 an excursion, organised from Miles Platting works to Goole, was enjoyed by about 1,600 people, with the company merely charging working expenses, between 30 and 40 pounds was raised towards the library and reading room. When the Newton Heath carriage works was built in 1876 a detached building was erected in Thorp Road for the purpose of housing the library. During the works dinner hour one of the men, elected each week, read from the current newspapers to his colleagues. At the end of each week the newspapers were auctioned off to the workforce, the proceeds going to the library funds. It is interesting to note that the Head Office Library was still operating in 1930, though whether any other of the libraries survived to this date is not certain.*

Overleaf: *An unfortunate accident, possibly due to over-zealous shunting at Irwell Bridge carriage sidings, when a carriage crashed through a wall and fell into Moreton Street in 1909. Recovery entailed the use of a heavy duty break-down crane and plenty of clearing up afterwards watched by an enthusiastic gathering of passerbys.*

LANCASHIRE AND YORKSHIRE RAILWAY.

HEAD OFFICE LIBRARY.

Rules & Regulations for the Working of the Lending Department.

1.—The Lending Department of the Library is open for the delivery and return of books from 1-30 p.m. to 5-30 p.m. on Tuesdays, and 12-30 to 1-30 p.m, and 5-0 to 6-0 p.m. on Fridays.

2.—Employees wishing to borrow books to read at home, must fill up an application form, to be obtained from the Librarian, which must be signed and certified by the Head of the Department in which the applicant is employed, and forwarded to the Librarian, who will issue a Borrower's Ticket, which must be produced on making application for a book.

3.—Borrowers are cautioned against losing their cards, as they will be held responsible for any book or books which may be taken out of the Library by the use of their cards, until the period for which the card is granted has expired. Lost cards can be replaced subject to this responsibility.

4.—Borrowers being transferred to a different Department must notify the Librarian within one week of such transfer. Inattention to this direction will render the Borrower's card liable to suspension.

5.—Borrowers are requested to use the books carefully, to keep them clean, not to fold down the leaves, nor make marks of any kind in the books.

6.—When applying for books the title should be legibly written down with the number affixed to it in the Catalogue, and it is recommended that a list of at least twelve books in the order wanted should be furnished in all cases of works in general demand, as many of them may be out at the time.

7.—The period of lending may be renewed, provided the book is not in request by any other Borrower. Applications for renewal must show the name and number of the book, the date of issue, the Borrower's signature, and number of card, and must be sent before the expiration of the time allowed for reading the book.

8.—Borrowers detaining books beyond the time allowed for reading will incur the risk of having their privilege to borrow suspended or forfeited.

9.—Borrowers returning their books are expected not to leave them on the counter, but to deliver them to the Librarian or Assistants, the Borrower being held responsible for books not so delivered.

10.—If any book be not returned in accordance with the Regulations herein contained, or if it be returned torn, cut, soiled, written in, or with leaves turned down or otherwise injured, the Borrower shall pay to the Company such a sum of money as will replace such book or the set of books to which it belongs, or be a full compensation for the damage or loss sustained by the Library. When a new copy of a book, or set of books has been provided in lieu of that or those injured, the person at whose cost the same shall have been so provided will be entitled to the damaged copy or remaining volumes.

11.—The Librarian is open to receive suggestions from Readers as to any books they may consider desirable to be introduced into the Library, and such suggestions will receive careful consideration.

ARTHUR WATSON,

January, 1921.   *General Manager*.

Book No. 2231

LANCASHIRE AND YORKSHIRE RAILWAY.

HEAD OFFICE LIBRARY.

**Period allowed for reading this book
SEVEN DAYS.**

No. of Ticket.	Date issued.	No. of Ticket.	Date issued.
69	27 JUL 1928		
2397	6 FEB 1929		
	1 MAR 1929		
2231	28-8-29		
2113	8 NOV 1929		
2940	6 DEC 1929		
279	7 MAY 1930		
2972	13 MAY 1930		

MATURITY ACCOMPLISHED

ELECTRIC LIGHTING
+ CARRIAGE STORAGE

Below: *An unidentified Aspinall Atlantic easesits train out of Queens Road carriage sidings under the watchful eye of the driver of a Midland Railway engine standing outside the Cheetham Hill carriage shed across the Manchester Loop Line. The LYR train will probably leave Victoria station with a residential service to Southport or the Fylde coast whereas the Midland train may make its way through Blackburn to its home territory beyond the Hellifield. Before Victoria station was 'closed', tickets were collected at the platforms extending along both the up fast and slow lines alongside the carriage shed. The bridge crossing the main lines carried the Collyhurst Connecting Line between the Irk Valley and Queens Road junctions. In its construction the far end of the carriage shed had to be removed.*

In conjunction with the British Electric Light Company, the LYR in 1880, experimented with the use of electricty to illuminate the station instead of gas. A generator was installed close to the Ducie Bridge temporary station to supply the current required for the eight arc lamps which were suspended from the station roof at strategic points and during the first few days of January 1881 experiments were made in an attempt to ascertain whether the illumination produced was up to requirements. This was indeed so inspite of the fact that the proposed reflectors on each lamp had not yet been fitted.

On Wednesday, the 12 January the lamps were lit in their final form giving complete satisfaction though it was not expected that the lights would be used regularly until a slightly later date. Prudently the gas installation was retained and, indeed, gas lighting was still utilized in the offices and waiting rooms around the station.

Unfortunately the electric light was troubled with unreliability for it developed a nasty habit of failing at just the precise moment when a crowded train had stopped at a platform. Feeling that the plunging of the station into darkness was a serious draw-

J.A. Peden

55

back the LYR, quite naturally, decided to dispense with electricity on Saturday the 11 March 1882 and the gas lighting was fully reinstated on the following day.

In a different experiment, electricity was used in the telegraph offices at Victoria station by Mr. Warburton, the LYR telegraph engineer, in which twenty eight of Professor Swan's incandescent lamps, powered by an 'A' Gramme generator, were arranged in the offices producing a "pure white soft light, brilliant, and yet inoffensive to the most delicate eye". However this, like the station lighting, did not give complete satisfaction and was dispensed with.

Undaunted by earlier setbacks and taking advantage of later developments the LYR in 1891, once again introduced electric lighting to Victoria station. A generator plant, consisting of three Mather and Platt dynamo machines driven by two converted locomotives, devoid of wheels, controls and indicators were installed in an engine house adjacent to the Hunts Bank head offices. Forty lamps were installed in four circuits of ten lamps throughout the station, interlaced so that in the event of a breakdown no part of the station would be left in darkness. Two of the dynamos were required to maintain the current necessary with the third on standby in case of breakdown or maintenance. By 1897 a further expansion of the generating plant was deemed necessary to cope with the anticipated extra demand for electricity in the station, not only for lighting but also for the increasing need for power for the ever widening range of electrical machinery.

The storage of carriages in non-peak hours was always a problem for railway companies as commuter traffic increased. At Victoria station the earliest carriage sidings were located within the train shed followed shortly afterwards by those sidings perched precariously on the incline at Newtown, several hundred yards from the station. As more sidings were required a site on the south side of the Manchester Loop at Cheetham Hill Junction was selected for several sidings and a six road timber carriage shed was erected in 1882. Probably at the same time ticket collecting platforms were erected adjacent to the two up lines alongside the carriage shed. Even though this building had to be shortened to accommodate the Collyhurst connecting line in 1904 the building survived until 1974. At the eastern end of the carriage sidings and utilizing three arches of Smedley viaduct, a gas making plant was installed. On Sunday the 13 August 1899 at about 9.00am a great explosion in the retort house resulted in the death of one man and extensive damage to the houses of a small estate which the LYR had been building over the previous eighteen months. It was reported that gas had been produced at Smedley for about fifteen years. Queens Road carriage sidings, laid in the fork between the Loop and the Prestwich branch, were used to stable the longer distance residential trains during the day. More carriage sidings were laid at Red Bank in 1884 together with a carriage shed.

These sidings were laid on land reclaimed when the cutting in which the Manchester Loop line passed was opened out on the south side, the spoils being tipped into the valley, the river Irk having been diverted to enable the extension to take place. Red Bank sidings were further extended at the west end bringing its capacity to 180 bogie carriages. Other carriage sidings in the area included Monsall Lane between Brewery Sidings and Thorps Bridge, Lightbowne at Newton Heath and Irlam adjacent to Agecroft engine shed.

Right upper: Although in something of a run down state the Cheetham Hill carriage shed still provided shelter for a number of diesel units. Adjacent to the siding outside the shed it was usual in steam days to stand stationary engines to provide steam for carriage heating before sending the trains out. The building was finally pulled down in 1974.

Right lower: Though the carriage shed at Red bank sidings is long gone the site of it can be easily recognised by the few remaining columns and the walk boards. The sidings which were opened in 1884 were extended to the west by the provision of several dead end sidings. By the time this photograph was taken in 1989 the four track Manchester Loop Line had been reduced to two from what was the site of Footbridge signal cabin which controlled access to the sidings. When all the sidings had been removed the site was utilised in 1997 by the signal engineers as a depot when work was taking pace for the re-signalling of the railway through Victoria station from Miles Platting to Salford Windsor Bridge.

Overleaf: This cross section of Red Bank carriage shed gives some idea of the construction of the building with the inspection pits to check or repair the vehicles and the narrow gauge tracks which were recessed into the wood block floor extending the length of the walkways from one end to the other of the building.

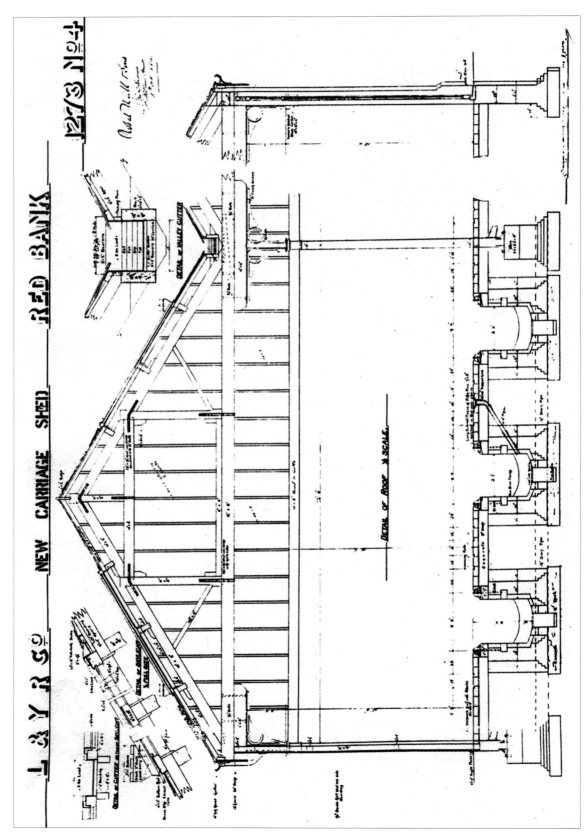

EXCHANGE STATION + LNWR DEVELOPMENTS

Below: *The plan which the LNWR submitted to Parliament for powers to extend their railway from Victoria station through Salford shows a slightly different line than was actually built though this was not unusual, quite often there were changes made before construction was started. From a point almost at the junction with the LYR line in the centre of Victoria station it was intended to pass over a new bridge across the river Irwell and alongside the existing viaduct before merging with the original railway a short distance to the west. Also a different line was intended for the approach road from Victoria Street.*

Whilst the LYR expanded both in long distance and local traffic the LNWR appears to have maintained something of a minor role as far as its participation at Victoria station was concerned for many years, particularly with regard to local traffic. As has been seen the station extensions of 1865 were of little advantage to the LNWR who had preferred a comprehensive rebuilding of the station as against the extensions as completed. The Liverpool traffic was, of course, of primary concern supplemented in the early days by services to the Midlands and the south over the Grand Junction Railway and to the north by the North Union

Railway through Preston. The Birkenhead Junction Railway gave access to Chester and North Wales from Warrington in December 1850 and also allowed the Great Western Railway to operate services to Manchester. In 1864 a new more direct railway to Wigan, and the north, was opened from Eccles and from this railway at Worsley the line to Bolton was opened in 1875. To the east the railway from Huddersfield had been opened in 1849 using the LYR between Stalybridge and Victoria and later the line from Droylsden to Denton and Stockport in 1882 enabled direct through carriages to run between Victoria and London.

In November 1877 the LNWR

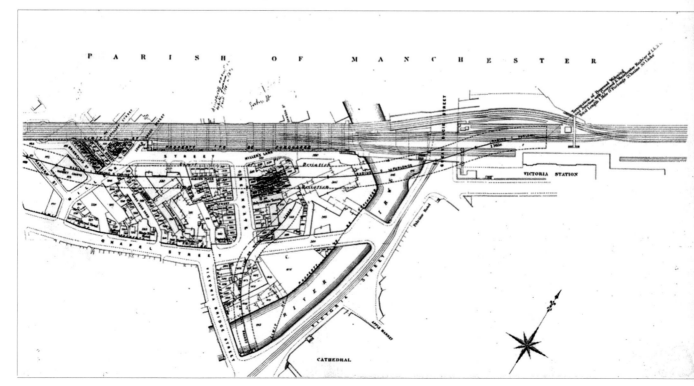

gave notice of an application for powers to purchase land to the south of their railway in Salford bound by Chapel Street, Greengate and Blackfriars Road with the intention of building a completely new and seperate station, also plans were made to widen the viaduct from Victoria to Ordsall Lane together with the railway to Eccles. At first, there was opposition from Salford Corporation but they were placated when it was explained that in addition to the approach road from Victoria Street in Manchester there

would also be an approach from the junction of Chapel Street and Blackfriars Road.

By September 1880 the main portion of the site, about 27,000 square yards had been cleared. The station which was planned to extend from the river Irwell to Blackfriars Road was to be built entirely on arches which extended from the south side of the original viaduct and by August 1882 a large proportion of the construction work had been completed and some of the platforms were being erected together with the foundations

for the iron columns which were to support the roof. At the top of the approach from Victoria Street, opposite the Cathedral, were the station buildings, comprising booking officess, waiting and refreshment rooms and other facilities and offices. This, the main approach, crossed the river Irwell and Chapel Street by iron bridges with brick arches between the two, at the top the road opened out to a wide circulating area fronting the station offices and was joined to the west by another approach, from Blackfriars Road, up a gradient of 1 in 28. It had been planned to build a bridge over the river Irwell almost opposite the foot of Hunts Bank but Manchester Corporation would not give their permission so, to enable vehicular traffic to reach the north side of the station, a road was built from the circulating area at the east end passing down and under the main lines and rising again to

Left upper: *Exchange Station commands a strategic position overlooking the junction of Victoria Street and Deansgate close to the Cathedral, always a busy junction. Exchange was a terminus for several tram services as well as those passing through to the city. The Cromwell monument was as good a place as any to stop awhile for a pipe of tobacco and a chat.*

Left lower: *In the mid-1890s the incline down from the Exchange station approach and up to platforms 4 and 5 was replaced by extending the bridge at the junction of Chapel Street and Victoria Street. The notice shows that thee two platforms were used for trains to Yorkshire and the north East, though there does not seem to be too much work for the two cabs standing by the notice. It is interesting that the circulating area at the station entrance was covered as there seems to be no reference to this facility. Road works in Chapel Street have blocked the tramway and are perhaps related to the man standing beside the open manhole cover.*

the area between and level with platforms three and four.

In June 1884 the LNWR announced the opening of the new station to be called Exchange on Monday, the 30th. and all trains which the company operated to and from Victoria station would arrive and depart from the new station. In fact, the station was still far from complete and even a day or so before the opening workmen had not removed the hoardings across the entrance and a temporary shelter had to be erected for the convenience of passengers. Because the footbridge was not ready a temporary wooden structure enabled passengers to get to platforms four and five. In view of the delays parcels continued to be dealt with at the LNWR office at Victoria. An extraordinary mistake was revealed when the station approach was to be connected to the roadway opposite the Cathedral when it was found that there was a difference in the levels of several feet between the pavements, so further delays ensued until the matter was rectified.

The widening of the railway from Victoria station to Eccles, actually it went beyond there to Barton Moss, was divided into two parts; that from Victoria to Ordsall Lane and from Ordsall Lane to Barton Moss. Stations on this latter section were enlarged and a new one, Seedley, was opened on the 1 May 1882. By June some sections of the new works were brought into use. Between Victoria and Ordsall Lane the existing viaduct was widened on the south side and was without distinction except that section between New Bailey Street and Irwell Street alongside Salford station. It will be remembered that here the original viaduct was supported on pillars erected along the centre of Booth Street. These pillars and another line along the south side of the street were sufficient to support the new viaduct and remain there to this day.

There were five platforms in Exchange station, numbers one and two were seperated by two engine release roads and three and four by a single track. Though platform five was inside the train shed there was an opening half way along the north wall through which a scissors crossover gave access to the through line outside the building. At first platform two applied to both faces with the north island platform being numbered three and four but this was altered to give each platform face its own number. From the cab stand between platforms four and five the road approach was altered to make direct access, at a later date, from Victoria Street, as originally planned, instead of climbing up to the level of the station entrance. To incorporate this alteration Salford bridge, over the river Irwell had to be rebuilt. A covered way, being an extension of platform three, enabled passengers to reach platform five (eleven) at Victoria station.

It is interesting to note that shortly after the emergence of the plans to build Exchange station there was, in Manchester, an active campaign by a group of leading citizens, headed by Henry Boddington, Junr. of Strangeways Brewery, which resulted in the production of several

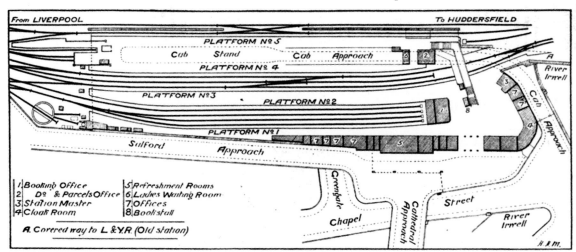

1. Booking Office
2. Do. & Parcels Office
3. Station Master
4. Cloak Room
5. Refreshment Rooms
6. Ladies Waiting Room
7. Offices
8. Bookstall

A. Covered way to L.&Y.R. (Old station)

PLAN OF EXCHANGE STATION (LONDON AND NORTH-WESTERN RAILWAY) AT MANCHESTER

EXCHANGE STATION MANCHESTER.

recommendations for the improvement of the area between Victoria Bridge Street and Victoria station. The plans put forward included the covering over of the river Irwell between those two points and the erection of a station of eleven platforms, the entrance to which would be built on the newly covered river. Quite naturally the pamphlet of September 1881, went to great lengths to point out the advantage of the proposals not only to the general public but also to the corporations of both Manchester and Salford and the LNWR who would have to be persuaded that the new station would be much more convenient than the one that the company was in the process or building. Although the proposal was rejected the new Exchange station came in for regular criticism for many years.

Left upper: *It was common to see trams in Victoria Street from several towns around Manchester such as Bury, Salford, Stockport and Ashton. The view is looking down the street towards Victoria station.*

Left lower: *The photographer has attracted the attention of every person on the concourse outside the booking office at the end of platforms 1 and 2 in Exchange station. The footbridge to platforms 4 and 5 stands just out of the picture to the right while the station entrance was to the left. At a later date a new booking office was opened at the station entrance and this building was converted into a waiting room.*

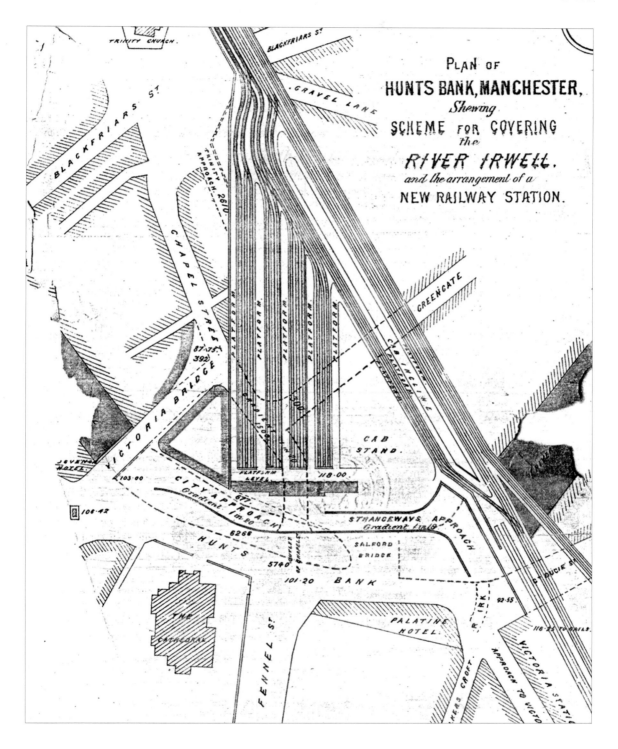

Above: *The plan of the proposed alternative to Exchange station prepared for Henry Boddington and his campaigners shows how the river Irwell would be covered over between Victoria station and Victoria Bridge. The station, if it had been built, would have had eight terminal and three through platforms, about 17 feet above the level of Hunts Bank opposite Fennel Street and have two approach roads. The plan appears in a diagrammatical form to explain how the station would fulfil the demands of the public for no doubt that layout of the tracks at the entrance to the platforms would have to be re-organised in a more railway like fashion.*

PARCELS OFFICE
+ CARRIER

Dealing with the extensive parcels and newspaper traffic at Victoria station was always problematic not only for the Passenger Superintendent's department whose offices were spread over several platforms but also to the general public who experienced much difficulty in finding the correct location from which to despatch their parcels or to receive them. In addition to something like one million general parcels and two million newspaper parcels dealt with each year there was a wide range of traffic which came under the heading of parcels traffic, including horses, carriages, dogs, fish, milk, fruit and vegetables. At the height of the summer season platform 6 (12/13), between 6.00am and 8.30am, became reminiscent of a vegetable market when loaded carts brought produce from Manchester's Smithfield Market to be sent to towns within a wide radius of the city, this traffic alone often required forty to fifty wagons each day. A similar number of wagons brought fish each day from Tynemouth and other north east ports and from Scotland, Fleetwood was not yet established as a major fishing port. Milk was dealt with to a lesser extent than in previous years as Pendleton took an increasing share of this traffic.

In the passenger superintendent's department some 130 clerks were regularly dealing with about 10,000 letters and 700 telegrams which passed through the offices each week under conditions which were not considered to be altogether healthy in the limited accommodation. Clearly it had become nesessary to remedy the situation and concentrate the diverse offices under one roof so a completely new building was erected in 1894 at the corner of Great Ducie Street and New Bridge Street on the site of the old fish market covering an area of 2,640 square yards of which the building comprised 1,905 square yards leaving 735 square yards of yard space for the delivery vans. A loading stage, 145 feet long, extended along the west face of the building, had an overhanging roof to protect the vans loading and unloading through the sash windows into the parcels office. At the side of the building a receiving counter for parcels brought by hand was entered from the foot of the approach to No. 6 (12/13) platform. The parcels office occupied the whole of the bottom storey of the building and communicated with platform 8 (16/17) by means of two hydraulic lifts, each nine feet by nine feet six inches.

The passenger superintendent's offices occupied the floor above the parcels office and were approached from platform 8 by two entrances. The well ventilated offices, built of fireproof materials, were heated by a high pressure hot water system and lighted by electricity. It was considered that the buff coloured brick building with moulded brick and stone dressings would greatly improve the appearance of the approach to the station from Great Ducie Street. On the opposite side of this approach a building for the Carriage and Wagon Department was erected in 1896 on a triangular piece of land and fronting Great Ducie Street there was a row of shops above which were rooms for the passenger train guards.

Opposite and following pages: The parcels office and passenger superintendent's department was erected at the corner of Great Ducie Street in the form shown in these drawings with the dome of the Central Control Office being added to the upper floor in 1915. When the station was 'closed' in 1913, the three entrances to the platform of the 1884 station extension were closed off though vehicular traffic was allowed continued access. The parcels office building was badly damaged in the blitz of 1940 and the upper floor was rebuilt in the form shown in the photograph.

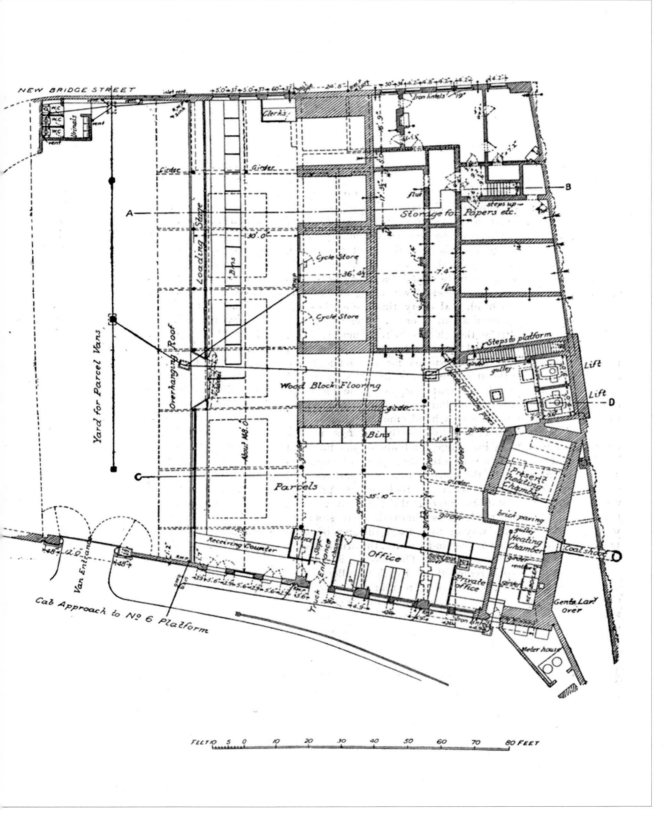

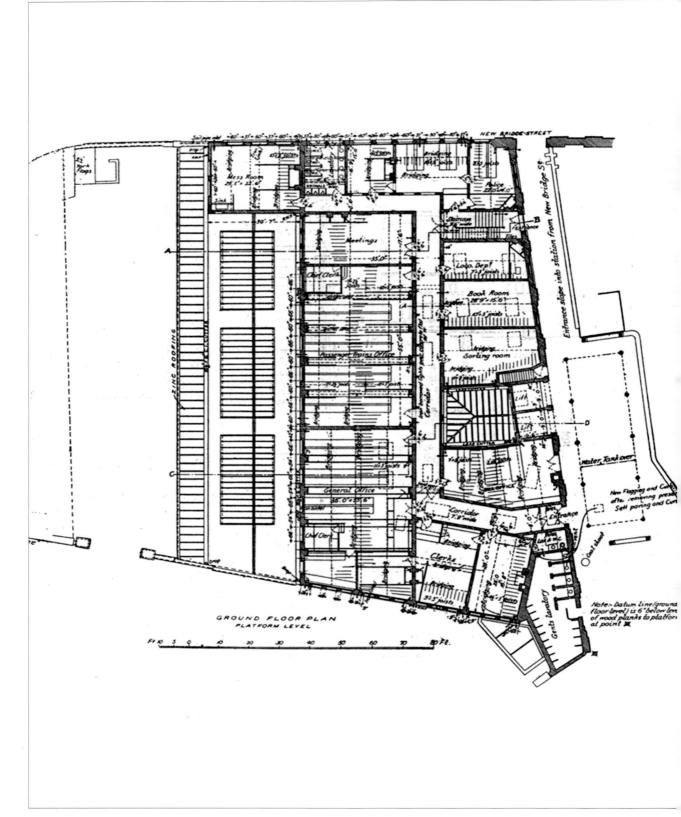

GROUND FLOOR PLAN
PLATFORM LEVEL

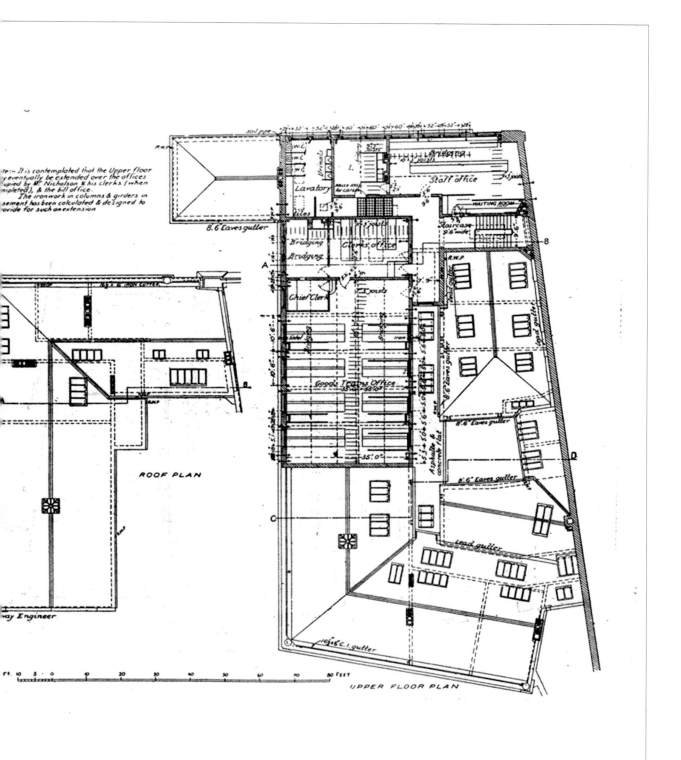

ROOF PLAN

UPPER FLOOR PLAN

PARCELS OFFICE
+ CARRIER

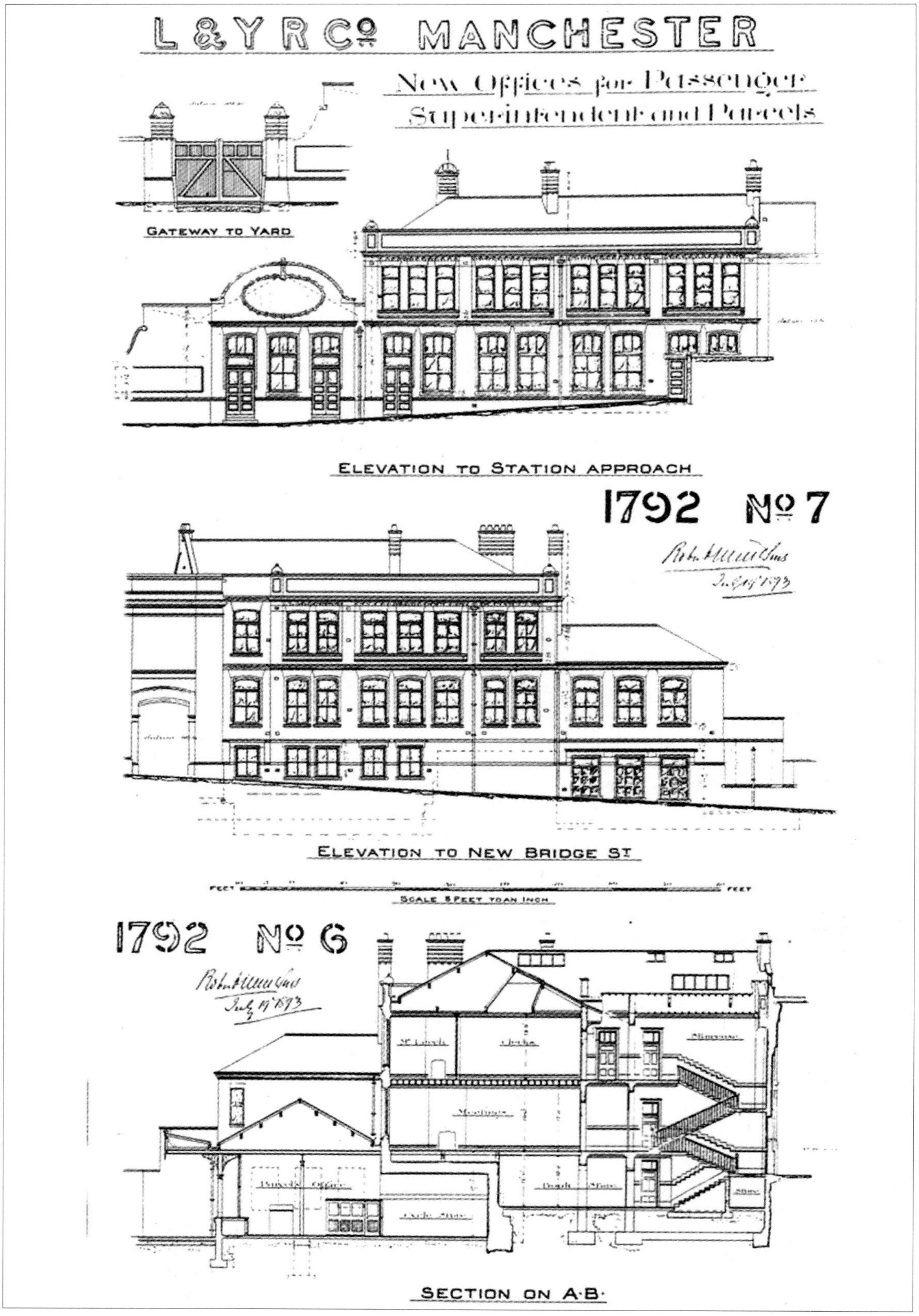
L & Y R Co MANCHESTER
New Offices for Passenger Superintendent and Parcels
GATEWAY TO YARD
ELEVATION TO STATION APPROACH
1792 No 7
ELEVATION TO NEW BRIDGE ST
FEET
SCALE 8 FEET TO AN INCH
1792 No 6
SECTION ON A·B·

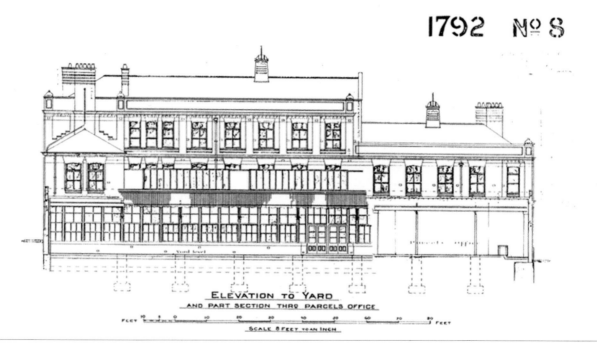

L & Y R C⁰ MANCHESTER

New Offices for Passenger Superintendent and Parcels

1792   N⁰ 8

ELEVATION TO YARD
AND PART SECTION THR⁰ PARCELS OFFICE

FEET   FEET
SCALE 8 FEET TO AN INCH

National Railway Museum

National Railway Museum

To facilitate the movement of parcels between the office and the various platforms an overhead parcels carrier was designed by the then chief mechanical engineer, J.A.F. Aspinall. The design, for which he obtained a patent in 1895, entailed the suspension from the station roof of a "track" along which ran an electrically powered trolley controlled by an operator who sat in a seat attached behind the motor. Controls enabled the operator to raise or lower a large basket from the trolley to the platform. Further controls enabled movement along the track at a speed of not more than eight miles per hour to which ever location was required.

The "track" was merely two lines of bars $4\frac{1}{2}$ inches by $\frac{3}{4}$ inch supported by inverted "U" shaped brackets suspended from the station roof. Running on four wheels the motor carriage hung below and between the rails. Sitting in his seat the operator was faced with four handles, the outer ones, right and left, controlled respectively, the forward and backward movement whilst the inner ones, right and left controlled the lowering and raising of the basket. The basket was five feet long, three feet wide and two feet nine inches deep and could be loaded with parcels up to a maximum weight of twelve hundredweights. Following an accident in which a man was knocked off a carriage roof loading gauges were suspended from the track at several points around the circuit through which the raised basket had to pass to ensure safety. The lower rail of the loading gauge was swivelled and

two bells attached to give the operator an audible warning if the basket had not been raised to the proper position.

At first, the 100 volts direct current for driving the three horse power motor was fed to the "track" from the station lighting supply and was collected by the wheels of the carrier from the rails. In due course, however, changes were made and wires were suspended on either side of the track with a tram car type trolley extended from the carrier to collect the current. Just when the change was made is not certain but it is possible the extension of the the suburban side of the station was instrumental for the alteration.

Of the three carriers one was usually held in reserve to cover for breakdowns and maintenance and the other two were used at various times to form a continuous service from 6.00am Monday to 10.00pm Saturday. Between Saturday night and Monday morning traffic was dealt with by conventional platform trucks using the luggage bridge and the hoists to the appropriate platform. A "station" was built on the same level as the carrier rails adjacent to the parcel office on platform sixteen. The operators climbed by ladder to the "station" there to await a call from a porter when a basket of parcels was ready to be despatched to another platform. Three operators, employed in the Electrical Department, were paid wages averaging about 25/- per week in 1926, that being the same pay scale for vanboys. One boy worked from 6.00am to 2.00pm, a second from 2.00pm to 11.00pm and the third from 7.00pm to 11.00pm, when two carriers worked simultaneously. During this period it was necessary for each carrier to be restricted to one half of the circuit from the parcel office. At very busy periods such as Easter, Whitsun and Christmas a fourth youth was engaged and two carriers were in constant use. When only one carrier was operating it was of course possible to make a complete circuit in either direction. Except in certain circumstances the operation of the carrier was confined to working between the parcels office and platforms 11 to 1, traffic to platforms 12 to 17 was dealt with by ordinary

Below: *The 'station' for the carrier was situated above the entrance to the office of the Superintendent of the Line and alongside a large water tank on platform 8 (16/17). With two un-manned carriers already at the 'station' and a third being driven to it with a loaded basket it must have been a quiet time. The 'station' has a guard rail round it for the protection of the young men who worked the carriers and out of view there was a ladder to get up or down.*

Opposite upper and lower: *These two photographs were posed to illus-trate the usefulness of the carrier. Both show the addition of the trolley pole method of current collection from wires on either side of the track. The vertical dark line to the front of the roof column in the upper photograph is one of the loading gauges fitted with bells at the a bottom to warn the driver if the basket was too low. Apart from showing the basket in the lowered position, the lower picture also shows the cage in which the overflow from the left luggage office was stored, further on can be seen the ends of carriages standing in the LNWR part of the station. Beyond the signal is a train destination indicator and news stand which advertises cigars at five for 1/-d and cigarettes at 20 for 9d. The double arm signal controls the exit from platform 5 (11) along the track which curves sharply across the LNWR lines. There is a short spur extending along the platform which was used to hold an engine waiting to relieve another off a train from Yorkshire.*

National Railway Museum

platform trucks though some assistance was given by the carrier when necessary.

In 1940 Manchester Corporation, who by this time were supplying electricity to the station, gave notice that they intended converting the electricity supply from direct current to alternating current. The LMS chief mechanical engineer instigated an inquiry into the feasibility of retaining the carrier as converted and reconditioned or its replacement by using conventional platform trucks. In a report dated the 28 June 1940 it was stated that "to dispense with the carrier would have a general detrimental effect on the parcel working" it was, therefore, recommended that the carrier be retained. In the event their decision was somewhat premature for six months later after giving useful service for more than forty five years an abrupt end came to the carrier when Victoria station was a victim of the blitz on the night of the 23-24 December 1940 which destroyed most of the roof at the west end of the station and the parcels office.

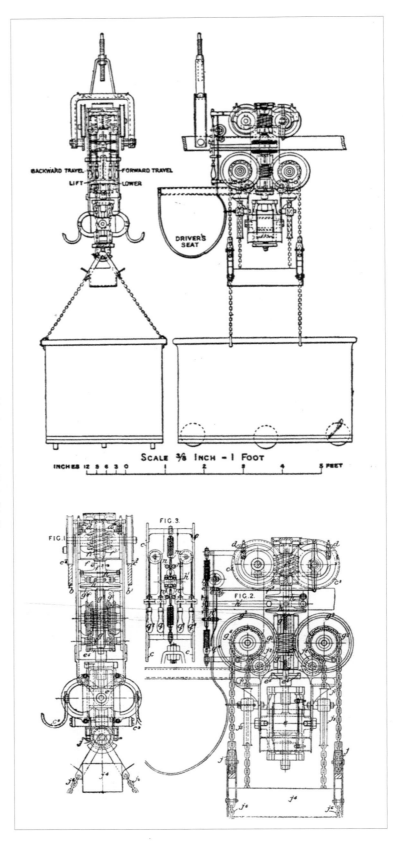

Right: *Details of the carrier and the drive motor.*

STATION EXTENSIONS

The 1890s heralded the dawn of an almost frenzied decade or so of construction and expansion to both the east and west of Victoria station culminating in a headquarters which would enhance the reputation of any metropolitan railway company and stand the LYR and its successors in good stead for the next half century.

As has already been pointed out, plans had been formulated in 1873 to double the railway from Victoria through Miles Platting to Thorp's Bridge but not carried out. Instead in the vicinity of Miles Platting much of the goods traffic was seperated from the passenger traffic by the construction, in 1889, of goods lines from Philips Park to the Oldham Road goods branch at Collyhurst Street and also from Thorp's Bridge to Collyhurst

Street, avoiding Miles Platting station on the north side and then by a bridge over the main line to join the Oldham Road line which itself was widened to the goods station. Provision was made to allow for the widening of the main line from Miles Platting to Victoria.

Authority to widen the railway was obtained in July 1891 and twelve months later it was reported that most of the land required had been purchased. By February 1894 the company was able to state that the provision of housing for those people displaced when their homes had been pulled down was almost complete and then it would be possible to start work on the widening. The tender of William Dransfield of £73,554 was accepted for the work on the 29 March 1894 and by August it was reported that

work had started. The widening together with the re-arrangement of Newtown carriage sidings was completed in September 1896 and it was now possible to concentrate local traffic on the southern lines.

In the meantime, the LYR had applied to Parliament in 1894 for an Act to build a railway from the south side of the incline, about half a mile from Victoria, dive beneath it in a northerly direction, then bridge the Manchester Loop line before joining the Prestwich branch at Queens Road junction, a short distance from Cheetham Hill Junction; additionally there was a south to east spur to the loop line between what would be Irk Valley and Smedley Viaduct junctions. The whole work would be known later as the Collyhurst Connecting Lines.

Right: *When the Collyhurst Connecting Lines were built they included not only the viaduct and bridge over the river Irk and the Manchester Loop Line to the junction with the original Prestwich branch at Queens Road but also a spur from what would be junctions at Irk Valley and Smedley Viaduct entirely on a brick viaduct as can be seen in this photograph. This enabled trains to and from the suburban side of Victoria station to avoid the complications of the junctions at Miles Platting.*

At Victoria and included in the overall plan was a major extension of the suburban side of the station to Long Millgate together with a connection from the lower end of the incline. To enable this to be carried out the company intended to extend the Cheetham Hill Road bridge by inserting a girder, 160 feet long, "in, along and above" the centre of the bridge and re-site the tramlines on either side of it. Not surprisingly the City Fathers were aghast at the thought, objections were lodged and at the half yearly meeting of the LYR in August 1895 it was reported that the clauses relating to the bridge and the

station extension had been withdrawn from the bill. Subsequently, in January 1896, the city council reported that agreement had been reached and that a completely new bridge would be built to replace the old and that Corporation Street would be re-aligned in consequence. However, they did object to the proposed width of twenty two yards when they, the council, had already declared a building line of twenty two yards for Cheetham Hill Road; the company acquiesced. In May, however, the council instructed the town clerk to stipulate that the old bridge would not be interfered with

until the new bridge was completed and that facilities would be "given for the verandah being placed over the footway on the west side of the new bridge in respect of the two openings to the station". In event this latter demand was not complied with.

Victoria Station Extension No. 1 contract for building the new Cheethem Hill Road bridge together with the diversion, arching over, and paving the bed of the river Irk was awarded to A.W. Smith and Sons and Senior for £89,594 in December 1898. The work was reported as almost complete in February 1901 and that the Corporation

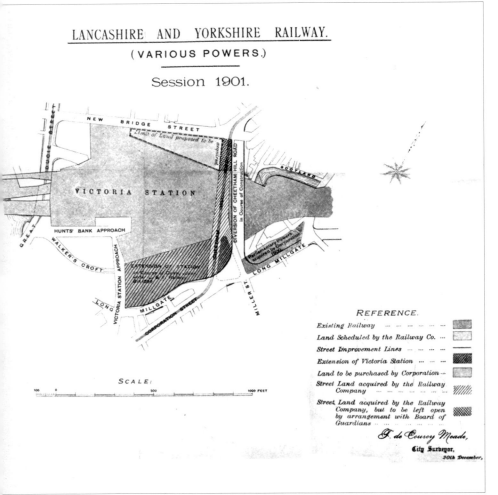

LANCASHIRE AND YORKSHIRE RAILWAY.

(VARIOUS POWERS.)

Session 1901.

REFERENCE.

Existing Railway ... ...
Land Scheduled by the Railway Co. ...
Street Improvement Lines ... ...
Extension of Victoria Station ... ...
Land to be purchased by Corporation ...
Street Land acquired by the Railway Company ... ...
Street Land acquired by the Railway Company, but to be left open by arrangement with Board of Guardians

G. de Courcy Meade,
City Surveyor,
30th December,

Left: Signed by the City Surveyor this diagram shows the land required for the extension of the suburban side of Victoria station, the new alignment of the Cheetham Hill Road bridge and the position of the existing bridge together with land on the east side in what is shown as Long Millgate but which was later re-named Corporation Street.

Opposite upper: Viewed from Corporation Street the new Cheetham Hill Road bridge has been completed and the old bridge fenced off. Lamp standards are in place and the tram tracks laid in readiness for the opening of the first electric tramway in Manchester which was opened on the 6 June 1901 with much pomp and ceremony.

Opposite middle: Taken from a different angle, this view shows the bulk of the new station roofs over the extended suburban platforms. Apart from a couple of carts there is no traffic to hinder the movement of the few pedestrians who are idly watching the men working giving the finishing touches to the bridge.

Opposite lower: Viewed from the lower end of Cheetham Hill Road the east face of the bridge in 1996 remains much the same as it did in 1901. The railed footsteps on the right are the more modern version of Jacobs Ladder leading down to Vernon Street alongside the river Irk before it plunges beneath Victoria station.

were laying tram lines on the bridge. It was opened for vehicular traffic on the 20 March and on the 6 June the first stage of the new municipal electric tramway system, using the new bridge was opened with due ceremony between Albert Square and Cheetham Hill.

On the 20 February 1901 A.W. Smith's tender of £116,486 was accepted for the Collyhurst connecting lines and this was followed by the contract for widening the incline from Lower Tebbutt Street to Victoria station, being the logical extension of the Collyhurst line and which was awarded to the same contractor in November 1902 for £60,629. The Collyhurst Lines were opened in October 1904 and the widened lines in June 1906. There were now eight tracks from the station for four hundred yards up the incline, six tracks for a further four hundred yards and four tracks to Miles Platting.

In the meantime the Victoria Station Extension Contract No. 2, which entailed a new station roof, platforms, fish yard and the removal of the old Cheetham Hill Road bridge, had been awarded to A.W. Smith for £75,529 on the 7 August 1901. Such was the progress of the work that it was reported in August 1903 that the first of the new platforms had been brought into use and work was proceeding in the removal of the 1865 bay platforms and building the new ones together with the widening and re-siting of the subway incline on platform five. This work was soon completed and the remaining platforms were brought into use on the 1 February 1904 when all the

STATION
EXTENSIONS

Below: *George Hughes, the LYR chief mechanical engineer, stands beside his inspection saloon chatting to the driver and fireman. The siding on which the engine stands is alongside the train shed wall of the original Hunts Bank station of 1844 in the LNWR half of the station. It was through this wall that a hole was cut by the LYR to enable the extension of 1865 to enter the station independently of the LNWR. The locomotive No. 731 was one of ten Newton class engines purchased by the LYR from the LNWR in 1873 before private engine builders intervened and stopped the sales.*

Right: *One of the George Hughes Dreadnought 4-6-0s powers its way out of platform 11 with a Newcastle to Liverpool express. These trains were worked in partnership with the North Eastern Railway, each company providing a train of its own stock but worked by their own engines in their own territory. In this case the train is comprised of NER carriages. Another intruder in Victoria station is the Midland Railway engine and train standing in platform 12 ready to follow the Liverpool train as far as Pendleton before going on through Bolton and Blackburn to Hellifield and its own metals.*

G.W. Smith

National Railway Museum

Left: *Not fully discernable in the gloom of Victoria station, the train stands in platform 11 and was probably destined for Liverpool or Southport. Above the train is the luggage bridge that was lengthened when the suburban station was extended whilst at the top of the photograph can be seen the parcels carrier track.*

Below: *Looking northwards along the suburban station concourse the boards showing the destinations of trains from the individual platforms stand out. In the distance is the dome of the grill room which was built on the site of the 1865 booking office. Again the track of the carrier can be seen completing its circuit before returning to platform 16.*

Opposite: *In 1900 J.A.F. Aspinall, the LYR general manager, commented on the inordinate length of time it took from deciding to extend or widen a part of the railway, proceeding to obtain an Act of Parliament, rehousing those displaced, contracting for the work and getting it completed. Given this diagram through Salford it does not appear to have been of great importance but when the work was completed there were four tracks which greatly improved the flow of traffic.*

National Railway Museum

platforms in the station were re-numbered, from south to north, one to seventeen. When all the platforms, sidings and through lines were included there were twenty five roads numbered from the fish dock which was outside the train shed parallel to Long Millgate.

The overhead parcels carrier has already been described and though it was operating efficiently there was also the additional problem of passenger luggage to contend with which caused enormous difficulties. The only mechanical assistance had been the luggage lifts in the 1884 extension between platforms six and eight and the subway in which luggage and passengers were segregated, in all other parts of the station there was a continual competition for space. To alleviate this conjestion it was decided to build a luggage bridge to run from the north to south of the station parallel to and east of the subway with the existing hoists extended upwards to the level of the bridge, each pair of platforms in the suburban side of the station were also provided with a hoist. The tender of A.W. Smith, £4,421, was accepted for this work in October 1901.

With the opening of the Collyhurst connecting line on the 3 October 1904 the Prestwich line services were transferred to the new platforms one and two, this was to prove fortuitous in the light of future developments at Victoria station little more than ten years later.

In general it was the practice to designate one destination to a single island platform, for example, Oldham trains would use platforms seven and eight and the appropriate destination sign was displayed at the ticket barrier. Usually Ashton trains ran into platforms nine and ten but the latter was put to various other uses including parcels and the replenishment of dining cars of which the LYR had several.

Whilst all this activity was taking place to the east of Victoria other improvements were also being completed to the west. As we have seen there were but two tracks between Victoria and Salford stations since 1865, though further west as far as Windsor Bridge there had been a third track since the late 1840s. In 1888 Salford station had been improved by the provision of an up through line which allowed express trains to pass slower trains which had stopped for passenger services

and the collection of tickets. This alteration had been made in anticipation of the opening of the new four track railway between Pendleton and Hindley on the 1 June 1889 and the introduction of a service of express trains between Manchester and Liverpool. The next logical step was to improve the railway between Pendleton and Victoria and an Act authorising this work was obtained in 1890 but before it could be started it was necessary to divert the railway owned Manchester, Bolton and Bury Canal which ran parallel to the railway for almost a mile between Oldfield Road and Windsor Bridge.

The main work which constituted the provision of two additional tracks along the north side of the existing railway was taken in two parts, that from Victoria to Deal Street, over six hundred yards, and from Deal Street to Windsor Bridge. The contract for the first part, awarded to William Dransfield for £85,255 in March 1893, entailed the widening of the viaduct on the north side to accommodate two new running lines and between the old and new lines two carriage sidings, Irwell Bridge sidings, with a

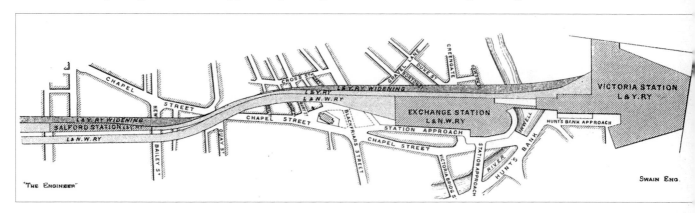

Above: *The booking office and station entrance at Salford was sandwiched between the 1865 extension on the left and the 1900 widening on the right. Steps and an incline led up to the level of the entrance from the roadway which was connected with New Bailey Street in the foreground.*

Below: *The highly decorated north face of the 1900 bridge contrasts strongly with the very plain south face seen in the view above. Beyond the LYR bridges is the original Liverpool and Manchester Railway bridge of 1844 and the widening of 1884. To the right beyond the bridges was the LYR Salford goods station whilst further on is the river Irwell.*

turntable at the east end. This was the scene of an unfortunate incident in August 1909 when a carriage, presumably pushed too far and too hard ran across the turntable and through the back wall falling into the street below.

There were new bridges to be erected, over Great Ducie Street and the river Irwell, this latter being a brick arch having a span of 105 feet, also included was the widening of the 1885 bridge over Great Ducie Street to accommodate another track and the removal of the roof over it.

Although the Board of Trade sanctioned the widening in January 1895 a decision was made on the 22 May to defer the completion until the October which, with certain conditions, the contractor agreed to. However, even though Board of Trade sanction was obtained again, in June 1896, there was still work outstanding. In January 1899 the engineer reported that the strengthening of the old viaduct had been finished, the contract work for the widening was almost complete and the laying of the permanent-way was in progress. The Deal Street to Windsor Bridge widening, including the enlargement of Salford station, was sanctioned by the Board of Trade in April 1900.

As the work was completed on the suburban platforms at Victoria so a start was made on the erection of a new block of offices along Victoria Station Approach from the original Hunts Bank station building to the corner of Long Millgate. The ground floor would be devoted to passenger amenities, booking

Left top: When the new extended platform was being built by the LMSR in 1929 to join platform 11 at Victoria with platform 3 in Exchange an additional support was required over Great Ducie Street. The arch of the original 1844 bridge can be seen beneath the widened bridge.

Left centre upper: This bridge is actually a widening of the bridge built in 1865 to accommodate the extension from Salford to Victoria. When the station was extended in 1884 it was necessary to widen this bridge to give access to the new platforms. Curiously, both the older and newer bridges were provided with roofs over the lines, no explanation for this has been found though it may have been to avoid frightening the horses in Great Ducie Street.

Left centre lower: The last bridge to be built over Great Ducie Street was that in 1900 in connection with the widening from Pendleton into the station. The design of the girders was necessary to give sufficient headroom for traffic along Great Ducie Street. On the left there was a row of shops between the bridge and the Great Ducie Street Station Approach, above these were room for the convenience of the passenger guards at the station. Part of the West Junction signal cabin can be seen at the top left.

Left bottom: Having a span of 105 feet this brick bridge over the river Irwell was the subject of some concern before its erection. To prove its suitability a scale model was built and when tested under load it did prove its soundness so the erection of the full size bridge was continued with and, as can be seen, still stands a hundred years later.

hall, restaurants, waiting rooms, toilets, urinals, retail shops and a bank. Most of the earlier premises had been demolished in 1899 but it was not until October 1903 that the refreshment rooms were pulled down and the licensing justices permitted a temporary timber building until the new facilities were available. In addition to the first class restaurant there was also a first class refreshment room adjacent to it and another for second class by the south entrance to the booking hall. Beneath the restaurant were the kitchens and first class beer cellar and connected with the kitchen were, in the 1844 building, a scullery, larder, wine cellar, waiter's dressing room, bottling cellar, bottle washing. cellar and a (silver) plate cleaning room. A cafe for general use, which included a large smoke room and a seperate room for ladies and children, was located at the south end of the building in the basement and reached by stairs in the entrance from Long Millgate. In connection with the cafe was a servery, kitchen, stores and a waitresses retiring room.

On the third floor at the north end were eight bedrooms, two bathrooms, a pantry and a sitting room; there were three more bedrooms on the upper floor of the 1844 station building as well. The rest of the floors of the new building were, quite naturally, devoted to administrative purposes. On the roof at the north east corner was a rifle range which, though it seems incongruous at this distance in time, was a reflection of the attitudes prevelant in those days when military prowess was encouraged in the form of volunteer militia though whether it was of much advantage in view of the conflict which was to engulf Europe a very few years later is questionable.

An early newspaper photograph, published in May 1908, was taken just after the scaffolding round the new building had been taken down, though there was much work on the interior still to be done, and there were as yet no fingers fitted to the station clock which faced the Hunts Bank Approach.

Left: *Certainly no architectural marvel, the new office block of 1909 by William Dawes was probably typical of the Edwardian era. The roof over Victoria Station Approach provided protection from inclement weather outside the two entrances to the booking office. A simple but decorative canopy covered the rest of the pavement almost to Long Millgate, along the front of which were displayed the names of some of the towns served by the Lancashire and Yorkshire Railway.*

Covering the pavement along the front of the building from Long Millgate an ornamental canopy was erected and along the front of it was displayed the names of cities, towns and resorts to which the LYR had services. Outside the booking hall a much larger canopy covered the width of the roadway giving adequate protection for passengers in adverse weather conditions.

On either side of the new booking hall maps of the LYR were painted on the white tile walls and it was whilst this was being done that, it is said, one of the painters was approached by a gentleman with some local feeling as follows:

Right upper: *One thing very noticeable is the contrast between the clean new 1909 office building and the blackness of the Hunts Bank offices caked with the soot and smog of sixty years. Another thing is the almost complete lack of road vehicles though the lorry in Walkers Croft to the right could possibly have been one of those built by the LYR for the War Department. The building on the right was the Palatine Hotel and is now part of Chethams School of Music.*

Right centre: *This scene of Victoria Station Approach probably dates from just before the Great War and the widespread introduction of motor vehicles. The stone work of the office building is beginning to turn from light brown to sooty black.*

Right lower: *A solitary policeman stands on duty with some rather sporty motor cars whose drivers were not likely to get a ticket for unlawful parking. The drinking fountain-cum-horse trough stands to the left and will stay there until the 1960s. The building is becoming decidedly dirtier!*

"Dost come fra' Rochda'?"

"No, why?" replied the painter.

"Well, tha's painted Rochda' bigger nur Owdham. Dostna knaw Owdham's bigger nur Rochda' an' Royton both put together? Tha'll get punced if some chaps as ah knaw fra Owdham cops thee doin' it".

At a company meeting held in October 1910 there were complaints that the booking office on platform 14/15 had been closed but it seems this was only a prelude to further changes. In 1913 the entrance staircase to platform 14/15 from the Great Ducie Street Approach was closed together with the ramp to platform 12/13, the latter being replaced by stairs and two hoists and the platform being extended over the ensuing space. An enclosure was formed by the erection of railings from the stairs to the booking office with ticket barriers giving access to the platform. Ticket barriers, which had been introduced to the suburban bay platforms when they were opened in 1904, were now extended throughout the station and platform ticket machines were installed. At the same time the Midland Railway booking office on platform 12/13 was closed. There was much apprehension as to the effects of "closing" the station which took place on the 3 March 1913 but the exclusion of "loungers, pickpockets and petty thieves" from the platforms far outweighed any disadvantages. It also relieved pressure on the several stations to the east and west of Victoria where tickets had previously been collected and enabled the closure of the ticket platforms alongside Cheetham Hill carriage shed. The ticket barriers as installed at Victoria station were of a novel design which enabled the ticket collector to stand in a recess in full control of the number of passengers entering or leaving the platform without causing any obstruction. The number of barriers at each platform was governed by the volume of traffic passing through and when there were few

National Railway Museum

passengers a single barrier could be used the others remaining closed. Side gates were provided to allow luggage trucks to pass to and from the platform.

One of the more unusual responsibilities of the station master at this period was to attend the annual meeting of the Victoria Station Lodging-house for Women whose premises in New Bridge Street was almost opposite the entrance to the station. Large towns and cities have always been an attraction for the young and vulnerable and Manchester was no exception. Those arriving without much money nor any suitable accommodation were soon noticed by the platform staff

Left: *Construction work is growing apace on what will be the booking office in the new offices at Victoria station. It will have to be completed before the older building of 1865 could be demolished. Construction could then start on the north end of the building. In due course a start will be made towards Long Millgate. The reason for the bunting was because of a royal visit to Manchester in 1905.*

Right upper: *The timber panelling on the booking office inside the station gives a rather sombre effect. The ticket office windows were usually arranged in pairs for each class with passengers queueing between two barriers then parting to either window thus not creating any congestion.*

Right centre: *Because of the number of passengers it was necessary to have control of their movement and this was especially so for platforms 11 to 16. Even so, long queues were a familiar sight at those ticket barriers which were introduced in March 1913. The Blackpool Tickets sign relates to the system of pre-booking tickets to the coast which was introduced at the end of the first world war. Notices were posted under Train No. Time and Platform and only those passengers holding the appropriate ticket on which was stamped the corresponding train number were allowed through the barrier.*

Right lower: *When ticket barriers were introduced at Victoria station they were of a novel design in that the ticket collector could stand in a recess allowing passengers to pass straight through without hindrance. A simple hinged bar at one end indicated whether that particular barrier was open or closed. In front of the barriers was an expanding gate used when the station was closed together with an adjacent similar one for platform trucks. For people not travelling or who wished to meet or see somebody off a new innovation was the platform ticket which could be obtained from a machine at one side of the barrier.*

National Railway Museum

who were instructed to give some assistance to the lonely traveller. Established in 1879 in New Bridge Street was the Female Stranger's Lodging House which became known in 1915 as the Victoria Station Temporary Home for Women and Girls. At the general meeting held in February 1916 the station master, Mr. James, stated that female railway employees, who had been given special instructions to look after girls and direct them to safe resting places for the night were doing excellent work in this way. The lodging house was converted into a temperance hotel in 1924.

The importance of advertising had been recognised by the LYR for many years even

Above: *Probably only the elite could afford to eat in such sumptuous surroundings as the Grill Room or the adjacent first class restaurant. The name in mosaics was easily seen from most parts of the station.*

Left: *For lesser mortals the cafe at the opposite end of the station concourse was more appropriate, even providing facilities which are even today not usually available. A separate room for ladies and children and even a rest room for waitresses was novel. White porcelain finger plates were usually found attached to the inside of the doors in ladies toilet at stations on the LYR.*

Right top: *W.H. Smith had for several decades the contract for selling newspapers, periodicals and sundry books on the LYR stations. This, one of several newsstands at Victoria, was located between the grill room and the left luggage office at the north end of the concourse.*

though it was mainly in the form of handbills and special tourist brochures. In 1906 a self contained publicity department was created specifically to deal with the wider aspects of advertising. Very soon an attractive range of posters was produced together with a selection of more than a dozen tourist guides featuring not only places served by the LYR in this country but also in Europe. Information kiosks were provided at seaside resorts and a novel advertising kiosk was erected at Victoria station, this latter was a hexagonal structure some thirteen feet high incorporating two revolving drums one above the other which displayed posters showing places of interest and train services. Other productions from the publicity department were bilingual notices aimed at the large Jewish communities in Manchester and Leeds, many of whom had settled from eastern European countries. In connection with the continental services timetables and

National Railway Museum

Right centre: *Advertising and passenger information always played an important part of railway activities. The LYR created a separate advertising department early in the twentieth century and a result of this was an advertising kiosk with the eye-catching system of two illuminated revolving drums one above the other rotating in opposite directions displaying photographs of scenes on the LYR system. There were also static panels advertising excursions and such things as sets of postcards.*

Right lower: *Commercial advertising was also encouraged. In fact, any vacant place was adorned with adverts such as above ticket barriers and on buildings in or outside the station.*

National Railway Museum

PASSENGER INQUIRY OFFICE.

National Railway Museum

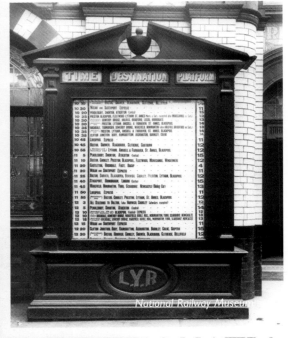

TIME DESTINATION PLATFORM

L.Y.R

National Railway Museum

NEXT TRAIN
WILL DEPART AT

11·40

AND WILL STOP AT

Left upper: *The passenger ticket enquiry office was an essential facility in any major station and that at Victoria would assist many puzzled travellers.*

Left centre: *Timetables took many forms usually a sheet stuck to a framed board with either LYR or Lancashire and Yorkshire across the top being familiar at ordinary stations. At Victoria more elaborate types were used including the roller blind which displayed a large number of destinations together with the time of departure and the number of the platform from which the train would leave. Periodically throughout the day the blind was rolled upwards showing the next sequence of departures. In this case the timescale covered a period of about two hours relating to the longer distance trains.*

Left lower: *In other parts of the station a different type of destination display was used. By using one of a selection of levers in the lower cupboard the stations at which a train would be stopping at was revealed on the display with the time of departure at the very top. A finger post could be inserted on either side pointing to which platform the train would be leaving. Note the medical cupboard at the bottom of the unit.*

Opposite upper: *In one of the last Parliamentary Bills sought by the LYR was a clause for the widening of the line outside the station from the east junction along the Manchester Loop Line in 1913. A number of streets would be closed completely including Ashley Lane from Corporation Street to Red Bank. Red Bank itself was to be diverted and a new road built to a junction with Cheetham Hill road. Those familiar with the area will realise that the new street would have been very steep and not very convenient. It was the street closures and the diversion that the City Council decided was unacceptable.*

Opposite lower: *From being a simple bride carrying a double track railway over Ashley Lane in 1844 widenings and extensions have given it the impression of a short tunnel. Even today it is possible to see the river Irk at the far end winding its way beneath the road and the viaducts. If the 1913 plan had been completed this part of Ashley Lane would have been closed off.*

brochures were printed in German for distribution in Europe.

Included in what was to be the last Act of Parliament to be obtained by the LYR in 1913 were clauses to empower the company to widen that part of the Manchester Loop Line from the west end of Red Bank carriage sidings to Victoria east junction and the entry into the 1884 extension of the station. This latter part would have had the effect of considerably easing the curves out of the station. Manchester Corporation were not happy with the proposals for not only would a large area of land be required but also the closure of the highway known as Red Bank and the bridge beneath the railway between Red Bank and the east end of Corporation Street. The LYR had proposed a diversion of Red Bank to rise up to join Cheetham Hill Road to the north-east of the railway bridge. It goes without saying that those improvements were not carried out.

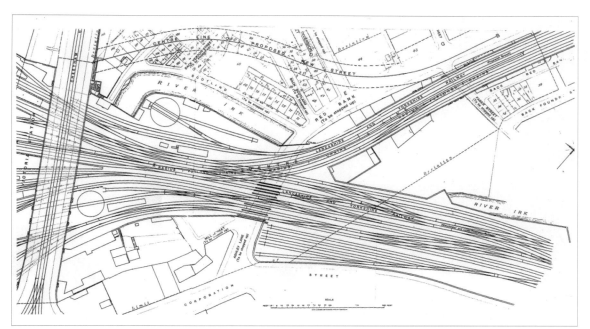

National Railway Museum

Station Plan: *The final stage in the expansion of Victoria station is represented in this rating plan of the 1930s. The next development would take place forty years later with the shrinkage of the suburban platforms and some years afterwards the closure of the northern part of the station.*

SIGNALLING
+CENTRAL CONTROL

Improvements to the signalling at Victoria Station East Junction were, towards the end of the 1880s, becoming necessary and as there were plans for the widening of the incline in the pipeline there would have to be parallel adjustments to the signalling. The major effect was the replacement of the two signal cabins on the east side of the Cheetham Hill Road bridge by a completely new building, East Junction, erected as part of their contract by the Railway Signal Company in 1889. This cabin had 108 levers and by the time the short spur had been inserted from the incline to the loop fast line almost all the levers were used. Further changes took place when the incline was widened in 1896 when, to cater for the increase in traffic, a new signal cabin, Millgate was provided a short distance up the incline on the south side of the viaduct. This cabin had sixty levers of which eleven were spare, at the same time alterations were made at East Junction cabin when fifteen levers were taken out of use and six were classed as spare. It seems likely that Millgate took over control of the lower part of the incline into and out of the bay platforms, the south lines, and East Junction was relieved of that responsibility though still having some control over the north lines on the incline, and of course traffic to and from the loop line.

The next phase of widening and station extensions, completed in 1904 altered the picture yet again with the removal of Millgate cabin to an elevated position between the north and south lines almost 400 yards Victoria station and the provision of a completely new cabin, Turntable, 94 levers, opposite East Junction cabin between the lines into platforms five and six. Millgate now enlarged to 78 levers controlled the destiny of trains approaching the station from the Miles Platting direction, likewise Footbridge signal cabin on the Loop line situated at the west end of Red Bank carriage

Opposite: When the Manchester Loop Line was first opened only the pair of tracks on the left or slow lines made a junction with the lines on the incline to Miles Platting. This meant that not all the trains from the 1884 extension could go up the incline or vice versa. To remedy this a short spur was laid from the fast lines outside the signal cabin across the slow lines to merge with the lines on the incline. Before the 1884 extension was completed the temporary Ducie Bridge station was located near the fast line roughly between the signal cabin and the Cheetham Hill Road bridge. Note that the semaphore arms on the gantry are of the two aspect type with a single red glass for stop and showing a white light when 'off'.

Right: Victoria East Junction signal cabin was built in 1889 to deal with all the traffic into and out of the station at the east end. Going through several transitions it would survive until 1962.

Below: Whenever alterations were made to signal installations reports had to be made to the Board of Trade who after consideration would pass the changes or require adjustments to be made. When the spur from the fast line to the incline was completed this diagram was forwarded to the Board of Trade for ratification.

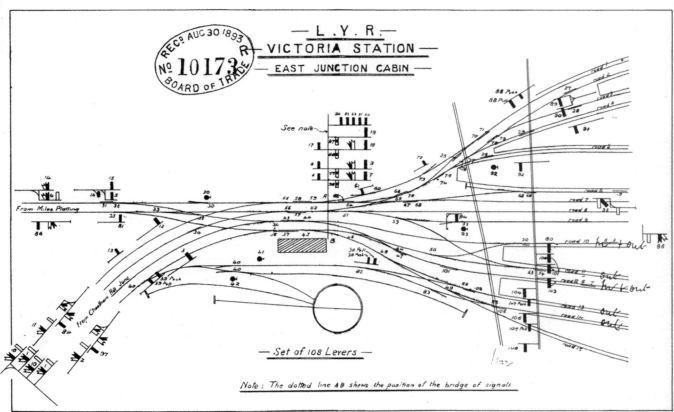

National Railway Museum

At the date of this photograph there was signalling for traffic to leave from six platforms in the 1884 station extension and to two platforms into the station both of which were bi-directional. The signal on the extreme right controlled trains into the bay platforms and another signal just out of sight indicated which platform they were destined for. The building on the right was the office for the inspectors who controlled the movement of trains into and out of the station; the white panels on the side under the windows were timetables. The practice of laying ballast almost to the top of the rails was quite common not only then but for many years afterwards. Because of the frequent movement of personnel about the station walk boards were liberally provided. The height of the signals is noteworthy not only on the gantry but also the single semaphore signals which can be faintly seen on the Loop and up the incline.

95

sidings controlled the double cross-overs between fast and slow lines.

For almost sixty years these signal cabins were to exert their influence over traffic with modifications to equipment and modernisation of signalling patterns as technology improved.

At the west end of Victoria widenings naturally influenced the signal installations but not to the same extent. The West Junction cabin located where the LYR and LNWR lines divided was retained but the cabin which had been at the west end of the 1865 platform was replaced in 1895 by Irwell Bridge, an elevated cabin similar to Millgate in appearance but having 120 levers located not surprisingly enough above the river Irwell between the ends of platform 6 and 7 (13 and 14). A quarter of a mile west on the north side of the viaduct was Deal Street cabin having 80 levers which, as well as regulating traffic, there were double cross-overs between fast and slow lines, also controlled the west end of Irwell Bridge carriage sidings which were located between the fast and slow lines, Irwell Bridge Sidings ground frame controlled the east end.

In the days before track circuiting there were two other small cabins inside the station itself namely Platform in an elevated position midway along platform 14/15 and Victoria Bays on platform 5/6, both were used to inform and remind the signalmen at the main cabins the state of occupancy of the platforms and the readiness of trains to depart.

Left upper: *West Junction signal cabin was situated in the fork of the junction of the LNWR line and the curve from platform 11 to what was the LYR line to Salford. It was opened in 1865 and removed with the resignalling of 1929.*

Left centre: *Millgate signal cabin, about 400 yards from Victoria station, was built in 1904 on the completion of the station extension and the widening of the incline. It replaced a cabin of the same name which was almost opposite the junction with the Loop Line just outside the station.*

Left lower: *With the separation of the suburban from the main line traffic each was allocated a signal cabin. East Junction taking the main line and Turntable controlling the suburban traffic into and out of the bay platforms. Turntable, because there used to be one to the right of the water column.*

Below upper: *Irwell Bridge signal cabin was the largest serving Victoria station having 120 levers. It controlled all the traffic at the west end of the station in both directions standing high*

above the railway, just beyond the ends of platforms 12 and 13.

Below lower: *Because of the difficulty of sighting vehicles standing in platforms 12 to 17 a signal cabin was built above the waiting rooms on platform 14/15 to work in conjunction with the signal cabins just outside the station. The aspect of the various signal outside the station and along the platforms informed the driver whether the line was blocked, partially blocked or clear. With the introduction of track circuiting its function became superfluous.*

SIGNALLING
+CENTRAL CONTROL

Right: The miniature electric trains used at the Victoria station school of signalling remained an important part of demonstrating practice until the school closed. As with many things introduced by the LYR it was improved and modernised over the years as can be seen by the use of a modern electric unit with an overhead collector in this photograph.

Below: All the functions of a working railway could be replicated on the model railway in the school of signalling to give 'hands on' practice for the scholars who attended the courses. In 1958 a party of members of the Manchester Model Railway Society visited the signalling school and as can be seen in this photograph some were allowed to operate the layout which is now at the National Railway Museum in York undergoing a complete overhaul before being used for practical demonstrations.

Opposite: A former LYR 2-4-2T No. 10912 comes off the Manchester Loop Line passing East Junction signal cabin and into the station in July 1931. In spite of the demise of the LYR ten years earlier, the engine and the first two carriages together with the signalling date from the pre-grouping period.

Signals and signalling were of prime importance for the safe operation of any railway and it was required that railway servants be cogniscant of the rules and regulations affecting this aspect of operation. The LYR, however, recognised that a more professional approach should be made in which staff would be instructed in more detail and that this could only be achieved by the provision of facilities specifically designed to accommodate this aim. So it was that in 1910 the School of Signalling was established on the third floor of the new offices at Victoria station. All grades of staff from porters upwards were encouraged to attend classes with the aim of improving their knowledge of railway operation. Shortly after the school was opened a large model railway was built so that practical experience could be gained by operating the model in conjunction with block instruments, working signals and full interlocking normally installed in signal cabins. The high standards attained by students was mirrored in the numbers of passes achieved at the prize-giving ceremonies held at the end of each course. Improvements and additions to the facilities provided were made over the years to ensure that the most up to date signalling practice was passed on to students. The school was nursed in its early days by Ashton Davies who subsequently became vice-president of the LMSR. His enthusiasm and expertise were rewarded by the high standards achieved. Ashton Davis was also involved in the development of train control on the LYR.

The need for overall control of train movements was recognised by railway companies from an early date but until the advent of an efficient means of communication this was not feasible. With the obvious effectiveness of the telephone together with the influence of American practise the LYR was stimulated into setting up control offices in 1912 at Liverpool, Wigan and Wakefield followed in 1913 by an office of limited scope at Victoria station but soon to be enlarged to become the Central Control Office for the whole railway. Though not the pioneer in this field in the United Kingdom the Manchester control office soon attracted a great deal of attention by its layout, arrangement and professionalism.

The central control office was established in the offices of the Superintendent of the line above the New Bridge Street parcels office. Erected in one of the rooms was a large circular display upon which was a continuous diagram of the whole of the LYR system starting at Liverpool and continuing round the room ending at Goole separated only by the entrance door. All stations, platforms, signal cabins, goods yards and sidings were shown on the diagram. The railway was divided into seventeen

E.R. Morten

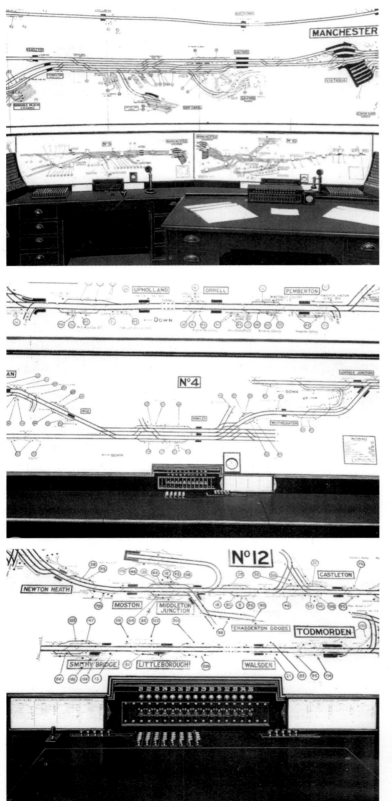

Left: *From his desk the chief controller oversaw the whole of the control room, the diagram and each section control display. Beneath the diagrams which were numbered from 1 to 17 the section controller was provided with a telephone switchboard through which he could be in contact with every signal cabin in his section. The LYR benefited from the American equipment as did their successors the LMSR who extended it to include other previously independent railways in their region.*

Opposite upper: *An unidentified Class 4 0-6-0 blows off steam whilst standing at platform 12 before leaving Victoria for Blackpool in July 1931. However, it is the dome above the central control office that is of real interest in this view.*

Opposite lower: *Following the destruction of the central control office and the use of the emergency office space was found in the Hunts Bank building for a permanent office. The senior controllers sat at a raised desk overlooking the section controllers desks along the length of the room. This office was used until the facility was transferred to Rail House at Picadilly station in the early 1960s.*

sections each overseen by an individual controller who, in some cases, had an assistant. On each section controller's desk was a small panel beneath the main display on to which they could record the position of each train which was then repeated in coloured lights on the main panel. By means of a telephone switchboard a controller could be in contact with every signal cabin in his section enabling him to control the movement of all trains. The senior controller and his staff in the centre of the office, having an overall view of the proceedings, could make decisions and issue instructions as necessary which included the distribution of locomotives, brake vans and other facilities essential to the smooth running of the railway. Though the main emphasis was on the working of goods traffic the operations, of necessity, were based on the passenger timetables. The equipment, which was mainly supplied by the Western Electric Corporation of America, was the most up to date and represented the modern thinking and approach of American technology which the LYR followed to its benefit.

Following the formation of the LMSR in 1923, an enquiry found that the L&Y control was of sufficient importance to be retained in its entirety plus the addition of certain sections from previously independent railways. So, the central control at Victoria station became one of the divisional control centres of the much larger company

The growing threat of war was casting its evil cloud over events in the 1930s forcing railway companies to prepare contingency plans to cover most

E.R. Morten

eventualities and one of these was the construction of a bunker at Victoria station to house the control office. Built as an enlarged and extended passage from the existing office it stretched beneath platforms fourteen and sixteen and was fully equipped to assume control should the main office be affected. In the event the

planning was fortuitous for on the second night of the Manchester Blitz, Monday, 23 December 1940, most of the west end of Victoria station was destroyed. The emergency control office was brought into use though at first only for essential work and though it was originally intended to accommodate a staff of twenty

eight it soon became necessary to increase that number to thirty six. This posed severe problems to health and efficiency of the personnel due mainly to the very confined space available with inefficient ventilation. In view of the importance of the control office to the working of the railways in the region the provision of a more permanent installation was given some degree of priority by the Ministry of War Transport. In spite of the demands made by the armed forces, authority was given for the supply of large quantities of telephone equipment required to fit out a new office. A large room in the Hunts Bank building, facing the station booking office, was made available and converted into the new control room. Along the length of the room were thirty two desks arranged in two rows of eight, back to back, the two inside rows were occupied by sixteen section controllers whilst the two outside rows dealt with other important work such as the distribution of freight and passenger rolling stock and unbalanced engine workings. Across the end of the room was an elevated row of four desks for the head controller and his assistants. Each of the controller's desks was equipped with a line diagram of the appropriate section. The control room was in direct communication with almost 900 stations, signal cabins, locomotive sheds and marshalling yards in the division together with adjoining divisional and district control offices. The new office was completely operational by the middle of 1942 which, under the circumstances, was quite an achievement.

Below: *With the threat of war increasing plans were made for the preparation of an emergency control office at Victoria station. The bunker was constructed beneath the platforms of the 1884 extension. When that part of the station was being demolished and cleared in 1993 part of the bunker was revealed.*

20th CENTURY ASPECTS

ELECTRIFICATION + THEN WAR

To counter the serious inroads being made on the LYR suburban traffic in Liverpool by the more convenient electric tram and to improve the longer distance services to Southport the company introduced new electric trains in 1904 between the two centres later to be extended to cover the railway to Ormskirk via Aintree. The success of this venture no doubt prompted consideration of a similar operation from Manchester where the company was experiencing the same problems as in Liverpool.

The route chosen for the conversion to electric traction

Below: The residential line from Manchester to Bury was chosen for electrification mainly because it was an almost self-contained stretch of railway with very few conflicting connections.

was that from Victoria station to Bury through the northern suburbs of Prestwich and Whitefield. This line was eminently suitable because, particularly at the Manchester end, there was no conflict with other routes for, as described earlier, the Prestwich line trains used platforms one and two at Victoria then climbed the south side of the incline as far as Newtown carriage sidings, dived beneath the incline and bridged the Manchester Loop before continuing the journey to Bury.

Announced to the general public early in 1914 the work was expected be completed by the beginning of 1915, optimistic it may have been but in the light of subsequent events it was a deadline impossible to keep. By the time the war had commenced such a considerable amount of the work had been completed that

the LYR was allowed to continue the project even though, of course, priorities were by then very different. However, by the latter half of 1915 it was possible to conduct trials and driver training on part of the railway only as the section between Victoria and Queens Road junction was not yet electrified. At Victoria station one of the two sub-stations required to convert the AC current supply to the 1,200 DC voltage was built together with batteries for emergencies and to supplement peak demand.

A partial public service operated from April 1916 which led to a full electric train service shortly afterwards. At Victoria the tracks serving platforms one, two and three together with the siding between two and three were electrified and also the carriage sidings just outside

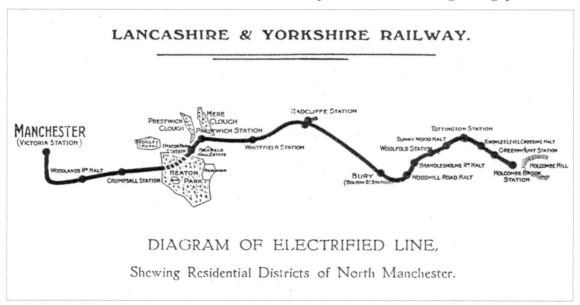

LANCASHIRE & YORKSHIRE RAILWAY.

MANCHESTER
(VICTORIA STATION)

WOODLANDS R⁰ HALT
CRUMPSALL STATION
SEDGLEY PARK
HEATON PARK STATION
PRESTWICH CLOUGH
MERE CLOUGH
PRESTWICH STATION
PADFIELD HALL ESTATE
WHITEFIELD STATION
RADCLIFFE STATION
BURY
(BOLTON ST STATION)
WOODHILL ROAD HALT
WOOLFOLD STATION
SUNNY WOOD HALT
BRANDLESHOLME R⁰ HALT
TOTTINGTON STATION
KNOWLES LEVEL CROSSING HALT
GREENMOUNT STATION
HOLCOMBE HILL
HOLCOMBE BROOK STATION

DIAGRAM OF ELECTRIFIED LINE,

Shewing Residential Districts of North Manchester.

Left upper: *A modern approach for a revolutionary form of transport with a female ticket collector standing at one of the new ticket barriers advertising the introduction of electric trains between Manchester and Bury passing through the 'Northern Suburbs'. The first women were being trained at Victoria in 1915 as ticket collectors.*

Left lower: *Coming towards the end of their working lives two of the five coach sets of electric trains stand in platform 2 and the siding between platforms 2 and 3 in 1958. For forty years these trains had given good service but by the end they were showing their age. Each five car set had three 3rd. class motor cars, one 3rd. class and one 1st. class trailer cars though the first class trailer was later divided into first/third class.*

the station by Millgate signal cabin which could accommodate two complete trains of five electric cars.

Had the war not intervened, followed by the re-organisation of railway companies in 1922 and 1923, it is quite possible that the electrification programme would have been extended to include the Oldham branch. In fact it was confirmed at a meeting in February 1920 that preliminary plans were being formulated and in May 1923 the LMSR announced alterations to the Oldham line timetable "to apply during the electrification of this section". In November 1924 it was reported that the work was to be proceeded with at once though as we know the conversion did not take place and the Manchester-Bury electric line remained in isolation.

Little over two years after the introduction of the electric trains one was involved in an accident on Monday, the 19 August 1918 when it ran into the buffers at Victoria. In general, however, there were few

mishaps until well into the twentieth century when on Saturday, the 15 August 1953 a very serious accident occurred at Collyhurst when an electric train to Victoria ran through a signal at danger, collided with a steam engine at Irk Valley junction and ran off the viaduct landing in the river Irk eighty feet below with ten fatalities plus many injured. The original LYR stock was progressively replaced in 1959 with BR stock which continued in use until the closure of the line in 1991 and its rejuvenation by Metrolink.

Of course, the Great War not only affected the electrification aspects of the L&Y, the loss of manpower due to the various campaigns for volunteers made serious inroads into the operational efficiency of railways in all departments and by the beginning of 1917 more than 8,000 of the LYR's employees had been recruited into the forces. One of the most noticeable effects to the public was the withdrawal of train services; in January and

February 1917 alone the LYR withdrew almost 300 trains from their timetable and fares were increased by about fifty per cent. Also there was the appearance in July 1915 at Victoria of several women ticket collectors and by 1917 there were 2,400 women employed in various capacities throughout the L&Y.

A new ambulance train built by the L&Y in 1915 was put on display at Victoria station on Monday, 31 January and Tuesday, 1 February before being sent to France. Consisting of sixteen carriages the train was divided in two and took up platforms nine and ten. There was an admission charge of one shilling the proceeds going to local military hospitals and also to provide comforts for the fighting forces. Another ambulance train was similarly displayed in November 1917 when the Lady Mayoress of Manchester formally opened the train for public inspection. At this time also there was a stall erected at the station to which flowers were donated for

Right: *The collection of flowers to be sent to local hospitals where wounded soldiers were cared for was encouraged at Victoria station with the provision of a stall for people to leave their donations. There was always a willing group of volunteers to look after the stall.*

Overleaf: *From the employment of women as ticket collectors at Victoria in 1915 women took an increasing roll in railway work. This lady with her shiny protective steel toe capped boots was active in keeping the buffer stops between platforms 2 and 3 at Victoria well oiled, note the protective boards along the electric collector rail. The apparent stopping power of these buffer stops reflect the fact that being at the foot of a steep incline every precaution had to be taken.*

National Railway Museum

distribution to hospitals and to encourage the recruiting campaigns a large notice board was provided with a display of posters

Because of the extraordinary demands put on the train services during the holiday periods during the war the LYR introduced, in 1918, a system of passenger regulation on trains to the west coast, particularly to Blackpool. It may seem something of an anachronism that during a war of such proportions there should continue to be large numbers of people taking holidays but these huge numbers of passengers clamouring to board the limited number of trains available created chaos particularly at Victoria station. The system, as introduced, required a passenger to pre-book for a particular train, a ticket was issued overstamped with a number which corresponded with the number allocated to

that train and when the allocation was filled no more tickets were issued. Instead of having to scramble for a seat only those whose ticket number corresponded with the train were allowed through the ticket barrier. In this way the severe congestion on the station concourse at Victoria was reduced to an orderly queue which, though at times quite long, did not interfere too much with other passengers and the working of the station. This system of passenger regulation, though subject to certain alterations was to continue for several decades making life so much easier for both the public and operating staff alike.

Prior to the beginning of the War labour relations on the LYR had reached a critical state with stoppages becoming more and more likely. The war effort on all sides had had a calming effect but several months after the armistice the situation

erupted once more culminating in strike action from midnight on the 27 September 1919 and lasting for eight days. At Victoria station attempts were made to maintain some semblance of normality and it was possible to run a reasonable electric train service. Services on the LYR were operated under the direct and absolute authority of the Central Control Office which assessed the availability of manpower twice a day to enable planning for the following day and also to prevent excessive hours being worked by certain grades of staff and for safety reasons no signals were cleared without permission from the control office.

In circumstances such as these there will always be the few who refuse to join any action and those who are always willing to break a strike by volunteering to do somebody else's job and, to cater for these people, a marquee was erected

---

LANCASHIRE & YORKSHIRE RAILWAY.

Passenger Department,...................Station, ...19...

A.................ex ....
consigned to you cannot be delivered owing to the **LABOUR TROUBLES.** Possession can be obtained at the Parcel Office here on surrender of this post card, and I shall be glad if you will kindly arrange accordingly early.

The consignment remains on hand at OWNER'S risk and expense, and failing removal and payment of charges due within six months of this date, it will be disposed of on behalf of whom it may concern, and without further notice.

Failing immediate removal and payment of any charges due, Perishable Traffic will be disposed of at once.

.............................Agent.

Left: A postcard sent to intended recipients of parcels to warn of possible delays during the 1919 strike.

Right upper: In view of the possible breaches of the peace during the strike policemen were drafted in from local constabularies to assist the regular railway police force. This group are gathered on Victoria Station Approach in readiness in case any trouble might occur.

Right lower: With a large number of non-railway volunteers drafted in to attempt to keep trains running, a marquee was erected on platform 5 and 6 close to the Cheetham Hill Road bridge to provide them with accommodation. The numerals on the signal arms relate not to the number of the platform but to the number of the road in the station which, including sidings and through lines, started from No. 1, the fish dock, and ended at No. 25, platform 17.

at the east end of platform five and six close to the Cheetham Hill Road bridge.

Probably the most significant result which came from the strike was the introduction of the eight hour day or shift for railwaymen.

There were two events resulting from the Great War which can be related here, one almost comical and the other profoundly moving. In June 1920 the Manchester Profiteering Committee had ordered the LYR to refund 2s 3d from a charge made at the Victoria station dining room. The Company in its successful appeal pleaded that the total charge made for a meal or four people had amounted to 12s 1d and which consisted of seven sausages, 6s 0d; four pieces of bread, 4d; six small cakes, 1s 9d; chipped potatoes, 2s 0d; pot of tea, 2s 0d. It was stated that the charges were fifty per cent higher than the pre-war period against an increase of 112 per cent on the commodities required and it was also pointed out that the dining room had made a profit of only two per cent in 1919.

The other event involved a moving ceremony held on Tuesday, 14 February 1922 when Earl Haig unveiled a memorial to the 1,465 LYR employees who had lost their lives during the Great War. It had been at the company meeting held on Wednesday, 11 February 1920 that a decision was made to erect a war memorial at Victoria station beneath the map of the LYR on the north wall of the booking hall. The bronze memorial, flanked by the figures of Saint George and Saint Michael, was arranged in seven panels which contained the names of those who had died. The overall dimensions of the memorial were thirty feet long by eight feet high.

At twelve noon a large congregation of relatives, friends and colleagues gathered to witness, in the unusual quietness of the normally busy station, Earl Haig rise and release, by means of an electric button the curtain which hung over the memorial. After the Bishop of Manchester had spoken a prayer of dedication buglers sounded the last post.

The event was made more poignant in that only six weeks previously the Lancashire and Yorkshire Railway itself had ceased to exist having been amalgamated into the London and North Western Railway on the 1 January 1922.

Over a year later to enable relatives and friends to express their sorrow by means of floral tributes a platform of Cornish granite and Connemara marble was laid down beneath the memorial on which were placed four large and seven small ornamental bronze vases into which flowers could be placed. When this work was completed the memorial was re-opened on Monday, 2 July 1923.

There were two other memorial plaques erected in the station, one just round the corner from the main memorial on the main concourse at the entrance to the goods manager's office to commemorate the ten members of his staff who died in the conflict. The other plaque was erected at the opening leading from the concourse to the fish dock through which thousands of servicemen passed to embark on a journey from which many did not come back. The inscription reads "To the memory of the many thousands of men who passed through this door to the Great War 1914 - 1919 and of those who did not return".

Below: For the war memorial unveiling ceremony at Victoria station a small leaflet was published giving the programme of the service.

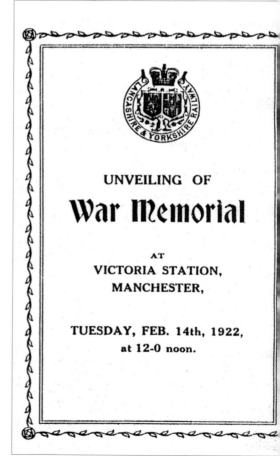

UNVEILING OF

War Memorial

AT

VICTORIA STATION, MANCHESTER,

TUESDAY, FEB. 14th, 1922, at 12-0 noon.

Above: As finally completed in July 1923 the war memorial comprised of seven panels listing the names of 1,465 LYR employees who lost their lives in the war. At either end were the figures of Saint George and Saint Michael. Below, on a specially laid platform, were four large bronze vases and seven smaller ones, three of which have gone missing. Each year since there has been held a short service on Remembrance Day to commemorate the sacrifice that those men made.

Below left: On the wall of the station concourse, just around the corner from the main memorial, a plaque was erected to remember the ten men of the Chief Goods Manager's staff who died.

Below right: Many thousands of men embarked from the fish dock at the Long Millgate end of the station during the war. It was to their memory that this plaque was erected particularly to the many who did not return.

RELATIONS BETWEEN THE LYR + LNWR

The dawning of the twentieth century brought a fresh and welcome change of attitudes between the LYR and its close neighbour the LNWR fostered by diplomatic meetings between the general managers, Aspinall and Harrison. Negotiations resulted in working agreements which helped to reduce the wasteful competition for traffic. One effect in Manchester was the transfer, from the beginning of 1905, of some Scotch trains from Exchange station to Victoria. However, no agreements could alter the layout of Victoria where the LNWR trains had to pass through the centre of the station and as far as the general public was concerned there were many complaints with regard to the inadequate communication between the

stations and the press were to agitate at regular intervals for a continuous platform connection. A report in 1905 seems fairly consistent in casting an unfavourable opinion of the situation which was to continue for many years: "It is no secret that the Exchange station is not a great success as a terminus, and still less as a through station, though internal arrangements have been slightly modified since it was opened, and the cab exit improved. In one respect the moving of the LNWR trains from under the same roof as the LYR at Victoria station in 1884 was a retrograde step, and no doubt if the work were being done today under the present friendly conditions a much more convenient joint station would be the result".

That relations between the two companies were less than cordial in the nineteenth century with regard to the working and development of Victoria and Exchange station was confirmed by G.P. Neele in his book Railway Reminiscences when he states that: "a little more concession, and a little more friendly conference between the two companies, could have produced a far more successful joint station".

Since the opening of Exchange station in 1884 there had been a few improvements one of which had been the widening of the road bridge over the river Irwell at the junction of Chapel Street and Victoria Street to accommodate a new vehicular access to the roadway between platforms four and five which had previously required a stiff gradient from the level of the station forecourt. A new retaining wall was, of necessity, quite substantial and the work was completed according to Neele in 1893.

Ten years later the LNWR were contemplating further extensions at the west end of the station which would have required the purchase of the Sacred Trinity church at the junction of Chapel Street and Blackfriars Street and the removal of the adjacent flat-iron market the loss of which would "probably not be greatly deplored by the general public". Salford corporation was opposed to the plans of the company as they felt that the pro-

posals would further disfigure the borough by increasing the number of railway arches which already abounded in that part of Salford. There was a suggestion that the arches should be masked by building shops in front as the GNR had done in Deansgate, Manchester when they had built their goods warehouse adjacent to Central station. It is doubtful that the opposition generated would have influenced the LNWR but in the event the extensions were not proceeded with and the west end of Exchange station remained as it was built for the rest of its existence.

In 1913 two proposals were published in an attempt to improve the surroundings of the approach to Exchange from the Cathedral. The first, prepared by the Manchester Society of Architects, envisaged covering the river Irwell and creating gardens on either side of the station approach and the erection of buildings to screen the less favourable parts of the railway property. A second, more ambitious, plan also included gardens covering the Irwell but proposed two new vehicle approaches and a much narrower central pedestrian approach. The new western approach would have left the Victoria Street end of Deansgate to rise to the station in a long curve, the second approach was to start in Fennel Street by the side of the Cathedral, bridge Victoria Street and reach the station forecourt by a reverse curve. The western side of Victoria Street would have had shops built over the reclaimed river down as far as Victoria station.

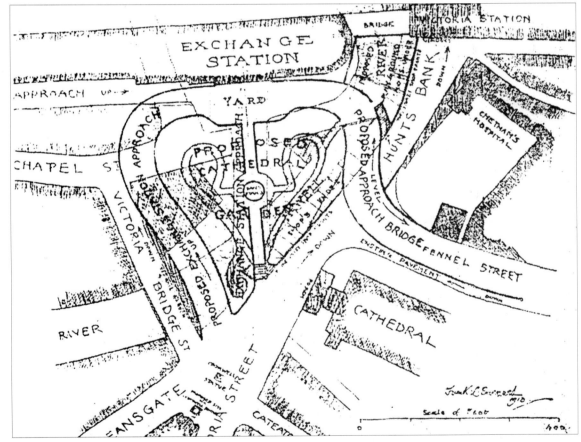

Opposite: *To accommodate the new platform between Victoria No. 11 and Exchange No. 3, it was necessary to widen the bridge over the river Irwell. The support was a steel lattice girder weighing 100 tons that, unfortunately, masked the rather graceful arch of the 1844 bridge.*

Above: *One of the rather more ambitious and flamboyant proposals to hide the river Irwell and provide an alternative to the staid and basic approach to Exchange station was this plan of 1913. With gardens and footpaths between the two curved approaches and shops above the river*

fronting on Victoria Street and Hunts Bank it would have, no doubt, given a more pleasant aspect to the area. Though the west approach was quite feasible the eastern approach would have been totally unacceptable to the City Council. Needless to say nothing further was heard of the plan.

J.A. Sommerfield

Left: *The middle section of the new long platform was adequately wide enough to cater for the expected number of passengers likely to pass between the two stations. The erection of a screen gave protection to the platform from the westerlies though it did prevent the enthusiast from observing train movements. West Junction signal cabin can be seen to the the left of the screen. Alterations to the permanent way have taken place in view of the closure of Exchange station in 1969 with a scissors crossover being taken out of commission.*

Below: *Comparing the two diagrams, before and after, there was not a lot of change to the layout of the tracks between Salford and Ordsall Lane stations and Victoria East Junction apart from the alterations from the centre of Victoria to the east end of Exchange and the provision of two sets of double crossovers between the former LYR and LNWR lines to the west of Deal Street signal cabin.*

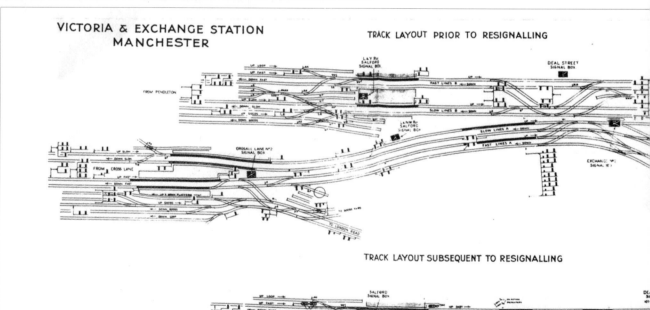

VICTORIA & EXCHANGE STATION
MANCHESTER

TRACK LAYOUT PRIOR TO RESIGNALLING

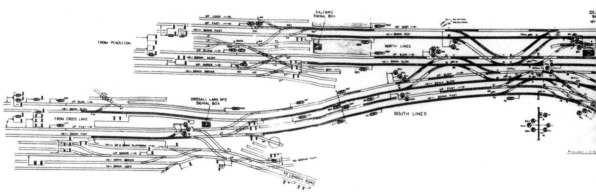

TRACK LAYOUT SUBSEQUENT TO RESIGNALLING

One of the vexed questions left unanswered by the two railway companies was the inadequate pedestrian way between the two stations. One commentator described it in 1906 as: "a piece of platform about a hundred yards long which looks like a little used siding" and an elderly railwayman whose memory was perhaps a little shaky said that "this bit of platform was all the station there was (about thirty years ago) and then, will you believe it, there warn't neither Victoria nor Exchange station, but just this little sidin'; they uses the old station for fish now - fish (!) and it used to be for folks and everythin'".

The problem at Manchester was that, apart from the junction in the centre of Victoria station, there was no other connection between the two railway companies to the west of the stations. This resulted in severe delays to traffic from the LYR line through Exchange when trains were standing in that station. To resolve this unsatisfactory situation a major constructional and re-signalling programme was embarked upon, initially by the pre-grouping companies. However, when the proposed union of the two stations was announced on Tuesday, 1 November 1921 it was cautiously noted that it may be some time before the

work could be completed due to the unsettled railway situation.

The work required the extension of platform eleven at Victoria to platform three at Exchange involving the removal of the old LNWR bay platforms and sidings at the west end of Victoria station and the widening of the south side of the bridges over Great Ducie Street and the river Irwell. For the latter a steel lattice girder weighing 100 tons across the river together with a parapet girder 142 feet long weighing 85 tons were erected.

It was whilst preliminary demolition work was taking place on the roof over the former LNWR half of the station that

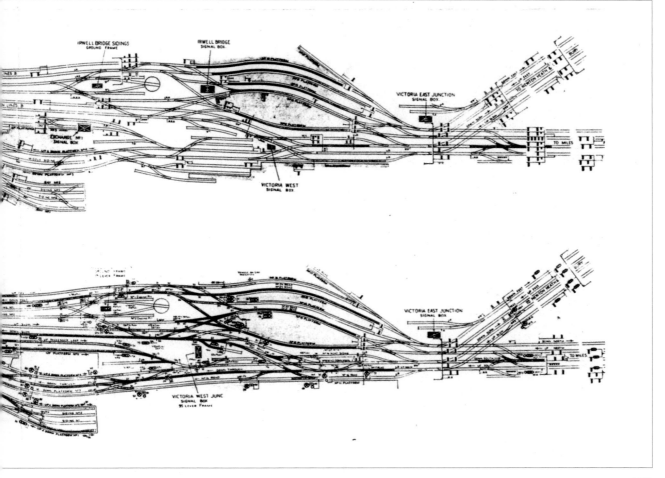

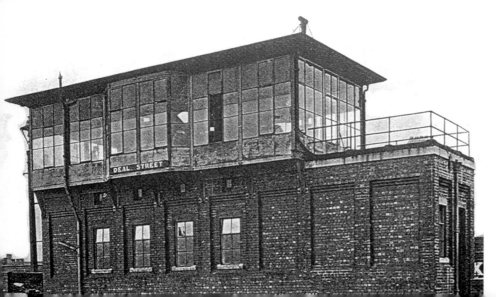

Left upper and bottom: *It would need rose coloured glasses to describe the appearance of West Junction and Deal Street signal cabins and even then words would not be adequate. Purely functional and without ornament the only saving grace about the two buildings was that the all-round view for the signalmen was, without doubt, unquestionable.*

Left centre: *For the signalmen, in this case in Deal Street signal cabin, the ease of operation must have been a definite improvement from the effort required in a mechanical cabin. The miniature levers on the console were of the three position type with the signal and point repeaters on the almost vertical panel behind them together with the block instruments, all within easy reach of the signalman. Above and behind the console stands the illuminated track diagram showing the position of all the trains under his jurisdiction.*

three men were killed on Sunday, 17 May 1925 when, as they were working on one girder, another being moved by a crane slipped and swept them to their deaths. The LMSR was severely criticised at the subsequent inquest for not taking adequate precautions for work of such potential danger.

The new platform, which was 2,175 feet, 2194 feet or 2238 feet long depending on which authority you prefer to believe, was completed in 1929 and formally opened on Tuesday, 16 April by the Railway Queen, Miss Ena Best, assisted by the LMSR deputy chairman, Mr E.B. Fielden, MP. It was of sufficient length to accommodate three trains simultaneously which could arrive or depart without interference. This was made possible by the conversion and extension to Victoria of the middle siding between platforms three and four in Exchange into a down, west bound, through road. The use of platform four for traffic in both directions was retained in the new arrangement. West of Exchange double crossovers were provided between the ex-LYR slow lines and the ex-LNWR slow lines and vice versa thus making it possible for trains in either direction to gain access to or from the two stations. The length of the new platform and adjacent track between the two train sheds was covered and along the north side a screen was erected of the type favoured by the LNWR which prevented railway enthusiasts from observing train movements beyond. One improvement that was not proceeded with was the erection of a new booking office on the site

of the old LNWR side of Victoria station close to the top of Hunts Bank Approach. No doubt had this been built it would have rendered those at Victoria and Exchange redundant by concentrating facilities at one point.

On the 10 March 1929 the new colour light signalling system was brought into use and the former LYR and LNWR mechanical signal cabins were closed. The area to be covered by the new installation was to stretch from the distant signals for Salford station and Ordsall Lane No. 2 in the west to the distant signals for Victoria East Junction in the east. These and certain other signals retained the semaphore arm which operated in the normal way but when pulled 'off' lights below the arm came on to indicate the aspect of the next signal.

The signals were mainly of the four aspect type arranged either vertically with, from the top, green, yellow, red and yellow, or in a cluster with yellow top and bottom, green to the left and red to the right. There were a number of three aspect signals which were similar to those above but the green aspect was omitted. The cluster arrangement was used at junctions and when vertical space was limited. The main reason for the reduction in the number of signals was the use of route indicators of which there were no less than thirty six, thirty of which could give eighty indications and a saving of fifty individual signals. The two signal cabins erected for the scheme, Victoria West Junction and Deal Street, replaced six mechanical cabins, Salford LNW, Exchange No.1 and No.2, Deal Street, Irwell Bridge and

Victoria West Junction. Irwell Bridge CS ground frame which had 29 levers was replaced by one of 15 levers. Whereas the older cabins had a total number of 332 levers there were only 188 in the new system and it was possible to reduce the working levers at Victoria East Junction from 110 to 85 and Salford LY from 67 to 59.

The two new signal cabins erected for the purpose were quite unremarkable and totally devoid of imagination in design. The upper floor had an all round glass and metal frame covered by a flat roof standing on a base of probably the cheapest brick known to man. West Junction was built at right angles to the railway to the east of Great Ducie Street giving an excellent view of Victoria station, Deal Street was erected between the former LYR fast and slow lines just to the west of Exchange station. Both had a console housing the locking frame running lengthwise with the levers, which were of the miniature three position type, about four feet from the floor on the raised front of the console and behind the levers were positioned the repeaters indicating the aspect of the signals and position of the points, above them where necessary were the repeaters for the route indicators. Just beneath the top of the console and above the repeaters were the block instruments gathered into two groups let into the facia panel with the bells actually on the top. Behind the console attached to pillars standing on the floor was the illuminated track diagram which was also provided with "train ready to depart" and "vehicle on line" indications. The former was given, understandably, when a train was ready to leave a platform by one of the station staff by pressing the appropriate switch which illuminated a lamp on the indicator which was cancelled by the signalman when no longer required. In the second case an inspector or other official actuated the indicator on the panel when there may have been an isolated vehicle which for some reason may have failed to break the track circuit and the signalman was thereby warned of the obstruction. This illustrates one of the problems of the early track circuiting when wheels with wooden centres sometimes failed to short circuit the track.

The electricity to operate the system was drawn from three sources, there were two of 400 volts three phase 50 cycle AC which were obtained from two independent parts of the Salford Corporation mains and the third, because another AC supply could not be obtained, came from the Manchester Corporation at 400 volts DC which was fed through a 40 BHP motor alternator set. The main contract for the work was awarded to the Westinghouse Brake and Saxby Signal Company to designs prepared by R.G. Berry and W.H. Moore both signal engineers to the former LYR under the direction of A.F. Bound, LMSR Signal and Telegraph Engineer. Mr Bound appeared to have been well satisfied with the results of the work for he stated in 1932 that during a period of dense fog lasting 120 hours in the winter of 1931 at no time were fog signalmen required.

What of the future, it is interesting to speculate whether the success of the new signalling west of Victoria station would prompt the LMSR to extend it to cover the east end of the station. The depression in the thirties and the war in the forties were probably the important factors which delayed any progress. However, it was reported in 1956 that work had begun on modernising the signalling installation at Victoria East Junction together with some alterations to the track layout, this latter being principally the widening of the bridge under the railway at the east end of the station by several feet with the insertion of two girders forty feet long to enable the easing of the curve out of the station. The new power box which was to be built behind the older East Junction signal cabin would replace not only that but also Turntable, Millgate, Newtown No.1 and No.2 and Footbridge. At West Junction and Deal Street the earlier installations of 1929 were modernised and improved to accept the newer facilities. By 1962 the re-signalling, by the Westinghouse Brake and Signal Company, successors to the company which had been engaged on the work in 1929, had been completed and was operating apart from some minor track work alterations which took place after East Junction signal cabin was demolished.

On the lower floor of the new power box were two 415/650 volt transformers and a 650 volt alternator driven by a diesel engine to act as standby in emergencies. Power to the signals was distributed at 110 volts and reduced to 12 volts at each signal. Of the two electrically powered compressors which provided air to operate the points only one was normally in use but in addition there was a diesel powered compressor for use in the event of breakdown.

On the upper floor of the signal box was a console upon which 466 two and three position switches were arranged on a slightly inclined panel and on the almost vertical back face were the various indicators, switches and buttons which were used for a wide variety of functions such as train describers, signal post telephones, signal lamp failures, adjacent signal chain indicators and power and air failure indicators.

Above and behind the console was the illuminated track diagram showing where trains were located by red lights at each end of the track circuit: Because of the steep gradients in the area visual and audible "train running away" indicators were provided to warn signalmen. Also because of the gradients two methods of activating the track circuits were used. For trains descending an incline the first pair of wheels would reverse the indication of a signal in the normal way but on ascending it was necessary to change the procedure and have the signal aspect reversed by the last pair of wheels of a train. This was because of the high incidence of trains requiring the assistance of a banking engine and the necessity of giving the driver of the banker a clear aspect.

By the late 1980s a reduction in the number of tracks, platforms and the closure of carriage sidings the importance of the power box was considerably reduced. There were now but four tracks extending from Salford through Victoria station to Miles Platting and the east junction was reduced from a quadruple junction to a double track junction with only the former fast lines from the Manchester Loop Line running into the station. The lines from two bay platforms merged into a single track beneath the Cheetham Hill Road bridge for several hundred feet then divided into double track before merging with the slow lines for the rest of the way up the incline. The Metrolink lines running along the route of the old electric railway were completely independent of the British Rail lines though there was a connection between the two systems for emergency use.

Right upper: The contrast between mechanical and electric signalling was very obvious, looking down the incline into Victoria station from Millgate signal cabin. The original colour light signal here would have been mounted on a standard wooden post. That signal has been replaced with a normal colour light signal.

Right centre: Of the two types of signals, a cluster of three or four aspects or in a column one above the other, the cluster was used as shown here where vertical height was restricted. The signal on the right with its route indicator controlled the routes through to Exchange station and off to the right to the former LYR line to Salford. The signal on the platform controls the platform line to Exchange and the diverging line to Salford, also with a route indicator.

Right lower: This gantry on the fast lines at the entrance to Victoria station alongside Irwell Bridge carriage siding illustrates the economy achieved. The two aspect up line signal with a route indicator and a calling on signal replaced a gantry upon which were no less than eleven assorted semaphores.

20th CENTURY PROPOSALS

For more than seven decades schemes have been mooted, discussed and rejected, to improve the exchange of passenger traffic between the several main railway stations in Manchester in which Victoria played a vital part because of its comparative isolation particularly from London Road (Piccadilly) station.

One of the earliest was proposed in 1912 when a planned underground railway was announced which would have started at Victoria with a circular route encompassing London Road, Oxford Road and Central stations together with a spur extending from Oxford Road station to the university. There would have been eight stations in all but the main bonus was thought to be the improvement in the transport facilities in Manchester.

In 1930 and again in 1936 Manchester City Council instituted discussions with the railway companies to consider the proposals of their Underground Railway Committee to link up the main stations with a tube at an estimated cost, in 1930, of about £700,000.

Between these two dates and following the success of the electrification of the Manchester to Altrincham railway in 1934 it was suggested that the electrification should be extended from London Road station over the former LYR lines from Ardwick to Miles Platting, down to Victoria, on through Salford to

Ordsall with, presumably, a reversal to Knott Mill and back to London Road. It was further suggested that the railway from Miles Platting to Rochdale and back to Miles Platting through Oldham be included in this ambitious scheme, harking back to similar rejected proposals in the 1920s.

Following the second World War Manchester City Council published a regional plan which would encompass all aspects of the community. The section dealing with railways envisaged a completely new station, "Trinity", being built between Exchange and Salford stations to which all services dealt with at Victoria, Exchange, Salford and Central stations would be transferred. By the time this plan had been digested the future of the national railway network was once more in the melting pot and with nationalisation on the horizon there was little chance of the railway companies committing themselves to any major investment.

In 1966 the ambitious Rapid Transport System was unveiled based on a similar network in America. Manchester planned to build on a north/south axis a suspended monorail from the airport and the vast Wythenshawe housing estate through the city centre adjacent to Victoria station to an overspill housing estate at Middleton in the north being a distance of sixteen miles. In a glossy brochure the projected monorail was shown superimposed on

photographs to show the effect it would have on the communities through which it would pass. A Working Party put forward several additional routes some utilising existing BR track and stations. After three years of publicity and speculation the project was allowed to slide into oblivion.

In 1970 plans for an underground railway to link Victoria with Piccadilly was submitted to the South-east Lancashire and North-east Cheshire (SELNEC) passenger transport authority for approval. This short tunnel was expected to be the central section linking two existing surface railways, that from Piccadilly to Alderley Edge and from Victoria to Bury and it would have had stations in the city at Market Street, Albert Square and Princess Street. British Rail must have been quite confidant of success for, early in 1973, they took platforms one to four at Victoria station out of use in anticipation of the underground railway coming to the surface in that part of the station. The Manchester to Bury electric services were transferred to platforms five to seven. The Bill for the Picc/Vic scheme as it had become popularly known received unopposed readings in both Houses of Parliament but heavy cuts in public spending delayed progress. In spite of a decision in December 1974 not to proceed with the scheme the Greater Manchester County (GMC), successors to SELNEC, was advised by the government to include the scheme in future transport planning. GMC had, by 1978, decided to scale down their plans and instead of the Picc/Vic tunnel they proposed a cheaper surface link connecting Salford station with Deansgate station by way of the Castlefield curve for which British Rail sought powers in 1980.

However, in August 1981 it was reported that BR were seeking powers for 700 metres of railway from Windsor Bridge to Ordsall and in April 1982 they presented to a group of interested parties their plans highlighting the Windsor Link which would have the effect of diverting from Victoria station many of the services hitherto associated with that station to Piccadilly and beyond to other destinations. The new stretch of railway was opened with the new timetable on the 15 May 1989. This short length of railway would be the only fruit of many decades of proposals to re-arrange the railways in central Manchester.

Top: *Early on the morning of the 10 December 1947 a train of tank wagons loaded with petrol ran out of control whilst descending the incline to Victoria station. To avoid another train the runaway was sent into platform 7 where, at around 25mph, it crashed through the buffers, mounted the concourse to come to rest between two of the columns supporting the office building just short of the booking office.*

Above: *A legacy from times past was one of the regular passenger services between Liverpool and Newcastle which would leave Victoria at 11.28 each morning. Here in 1956, Jubilee No. 45717 Dauntless has just pulled out of platform 13 for its journey to the north east.*

Left: *Even by the middle of the 1950s there was not much obvious change to the station concourse. Only the newstand and the mode of dress positively identify the scene as post war.*

121

J. Peden

CHANGES, DECLINE + METROLINK

Changes by the LMSR to Victoria and Exchange stations, apart from the re-signalling work in 1929, were not of an extensive nature. There was little change to train services for many years though the headquarters were replaced by divisional offices and there was but one station-master to oversee both stations.

In 1921 a new Benn and Cronin combined train indicator and advertisement was erected opposite the booking office at Victoria to replace a similar installation. At least these were an improvement on the timetables displayed in 1908 where strips of glass were fixed across the display in an apparent random fashion. However, an inspector was forthcoming in his explanation that "people were fond of taking a bit of pencil and tracing their train across the sheet, the result is that the timetable gets to look more like a drawing lesson and other folks can't make out the figures".

To allow engine smoke to escape more quickly the overall roof spanning the tracks between platforms eleven and twelve was removed in 1935 and a new canopy along platform eleven was erected together with a protecting screen along the line of platform twelve.

Two years later another section of roof at the station was removed but in more dramatic circumstances. On the morning of Friday, 21 May 1937 a single deck bus running on the Sheffield to Manchester service entered Victoria Station Approach from Todd Street skidded into a stationary taxi-cab then veered across the road and crashed into one of the columns which supported the overall roof over the road. The end of the canopy then fell onto the roof of the bus. A shop-keeper said that he saw the bus "skid into the taxi-cab but to see the canopy fall was astounding". Fortunately, there were but two women passengers on the bus at the time and they were only slightly injured, the driver and conductor were treated for shock. Railway and city police were soon on the scene and barriers were erected to keep back the onlookers. Whilst workmen were preparing to clear the damage the bus was being slowly crushed under the weight of the canopy. Because the canopy had been erected in five sections it was possible to remove the damaged portion leaving the remainder intact for almost thirty years before being completely removed in the early 1960s. To protect passengers from the elements an austere verandah was erected over the pavement in front of the booking office which contrasted markedly with the ornamental verandah which to this day boasts the names of towns, cities and resorts served by the former LYR. Also, during 1937 a tannoy public address system was installed throughout the station.

On the nights of Sunday and Monday, the 22 and 23 of December 1940 Manchester and Salford suffered major attacks by the Luftwaffe with large areas devastated. On the Sunday night the station offices and the east end of the station roof at Exchange sustained major damage with one bomb penetrating the bridge over Greengate and destroying a bus beneath which had sought refuge from the air raid. The seventy foot span roof at the east end of platforms one and two collapsed when high explosive and incendiary bombs exploded destroying one of the twenty one inch diameter cast iron columns. During the days that followed work continued to clear the debris and the lines through the station. Girders were found to rebuild the bridge over Greengate, the cast iron column was replaced by a steel plated stanchion and the damaged platforms were repaired with pre-cast concrete slabs. Because of the dangerous condition of the station offices it was necessary to borrow telescopic fire escape equipment from the corporation fire brigade to pull down the remains of the building. Meanwhile, an emergency entrance and exit was arranged to enable passengers to use the station, though it was about three months before the normal entrance was re-instated together with the repaired platforms.

The following night, Monday, 23 December it was the turn of

National Railway Museum

Above: The Benn and Cronin train indicator was a considerable improvement on the usual sheet timetables which could be easily defaced by pencil lines being drawn across them. Departure times to all main stations were distributed across the display with a lower panel for Sunday services. As in the present day, advertising revenue contributed towards the installation and as can be seen advertising was also distributed around the station as well. Time was not neglected with the large double faced clock over the concourse together with another attached to the roof column facing the suburban platforms, there was no excuse for being late!

Right: With canopy roof firmly embedded in the roof of a single deck bus in 1937 much work was entailed in having it extricated without causing even more damage. Once the section of the roof was dismantled the rest of the canopy remained in place until about 1960. The bus service was operated by Sheffield Corporation and continued to come to Manchester for a few more decades though the terminus was moved to other locations.

Above: *Exchange station suffered serious bomb damage on the night of the 22 December 1940. As well as the roof the station building on the right was also badly damaged together with a number of carriages in the station at the time. Though the roof was repaired the station offices were not rebuilt.*

Left: *One of the bombs penetrated the arch over Greengate. By great misfortune a bus which had entered the arch in an attempt to avoid the air raid suffered a direct hit with loss of life.*

Below *The night after the Exchange station raid it was the turn of Victoria station to suffer during the night of the 23 December. There was serious damage to the 1884 extension between the station master's office and Great Ducie Street. Incendiary and high explosive destroyed a large part of the roof and the parcels office. This part of the station had to be closed for some time whilst demolition took place.*

Victoria to be the target of a further raid. As on the previous attack incendiary and high explosive bombs were used destroying a large part of the roof over platforms twelve to sixteen to the west of the subway together with the buildings at the corner of Great Ducie Street and New Bridge Street housing the parcels office and over head carrier, the district control office and the district superintendents offices. Because the station roof was reduced to a mass of twisted metal and broken glass the six platforms had to be closed for several days until the debris could be removed. Oxy-acetylene equipment was brought in to cut away the damaged girders and a military trestle was used to support part of the roof whilst work continued. Some of the cast iron roof columns which had been fractured by the heat were strengthened with mild steel straps. Because of certain difficulties the damaged walls of the station had to be taken down brick by brick. The steel framework of the dome above the control office though intact, was in a dangerous position which required lowering slowly with the aid of hydraulic jacks whilst the supporting walls were removed. When safe the dome itself was cut up into manageable sections. The emergency control office was, luckily, spared and as we have seen already was brought into use though only for essential work.

A few days after the raid sufficient debris had been removed to enable two platforms to be re-opened followed soon afterwards by two more. The remaining platforms were retained by the engineering department for some time to enable them to continue the repair work. The parcels office was rebuilt in a modified form and a small ticket collector's office was built close to the end of platform seventeen but no attempt was made to replace the destroyed roof and that end of the station remained open to the elements until 1993 when the whole site was cleared for redevelopment.

In January 1953 plans were announced to provide a new frontage to Exchange station but there was little change until 1969 when the station was closed and all traffic transferred to Victoria station.

A new telephone exchange was installed at Victoria station in 1951 to replace the older equipment which dated back to 1923. A new manual exchange was completed on the 10 June then the older exchange was removed and the new 450 line automatic exchange installed and connected up on the 12 August. Because of the lack of space the new exchange had had to be built at the same location as the old and this meant that for over two months all calls had to be handled by the manual switchboard. The new exchange was manufactured and installed by the General Electric Company. Fax machines are not necessarily the most modern innovation that some people would have us believe for in April 1955 a Desk Fax telewriter apparatus was provided in the offices at Victoria station. Primitive though it may have been it was soon dealing with over 200 letters a day between the district headquarters and the several goods depots in the region.

During the early 1960s most of the administrative work was transferred from Victoria station to modern accommodation at Piccadilly station leaving the offices on Hunts Bank empty. In March 1975 it was reported that plans were being considered for the inclusion of Victoria station in a wider scheme of modernisation in the region. Six months later, in August, a fire badly damaged the Hunts Bank offices and, despite a campaign by the Manchester Victorian Society, their complete demolition and landscaping of the site was included in more plans announced in November 1977 which envisaged the cleaning of the 1909 office building facade and the original 1844 Hunts Bank station building together with improvements to the facilities for bus passengers who used the station.

In June 1978 the roof over the fish dock was removed and a start was made on the demolition of the Hunts Bank offices, this latter work being completed in February 1979. Further demolition work took place in 1981 when the disused Swan Hotel and the Phoenix corn mill at the corner of Long Millgate and Victoria Station Approach were razed to the ground, not railway property but part of the overall scheme of improvements.

In February 1982 the asphalt covered timber concourse was taken up revealing the brick pillars which supported the flooring and after filling in the surface was laid with tiles. Early in 1984 about two thirds of the station roof covering what

Left: *The area covered by Victoria station can be judged from this photograph taken from the nearby multistory building. The main changes have been to the various roofs in the station with those to the east and west of the 1884 extension being removed and those over the bay platforms being foreshortened. At the east end above the roof can be seen what remained of the Workhouse premises and at the west end the rebuilt parcels office.*

Below: *The roof over platforms 12 to 17 was removed in preparation for the construction of a sports arena over Christmas and New Year 1992/93. Already concrete columns which will extend along the new part of the station have reached the first floor. The parcel office at the corner of Great Ducie Street and New Bridge Street, now renamed Trinity Way, was demolished in February 1993. The subway was also closed in 1993 and an emergency footbridge erected in its place. Platforms 14, 15 and 16 continued to be used until November 1993 when traffic was transferred to platform 11 and the new platform 12.*

had been platforms one to three and the associated train shed wall was removed, the remaining roof being buttressed by steel girders. The ticket barriers which extended along the concourse from platform one to ten were removed in 1985 and entry to the few remaining platforms was concentrated at one point opposite the booking office.

The last eyesore to survive, the row of shops on Victoria Station Approach, was destroyed by fire in May 1980, the debris being cleared away in November. The whole of the area bounded by Victoria Station Approach, Hunts Bank and Walkers Croft was grassed over with a car park off Walkers Croft and a retail shop erected above the entrance to the railwaymen's staff club on Victoria Station Approach. Television screens were installed giving up-to-date information on train movements and "street market" stalls were introduced to give colour and atmosphere to the station

concourse but unfortunately they were short lived and soon disappeared.

With the opening of the Windsor Link in 1989 the timetable which came into effect in May revealed a considerable number of trains being transferred from Victoria to Piccadilly and this, followed by the Metrolink Project, created a situation in which there would be a considerable amount of spare land coming available at Victoria station.

The depot and offices for the Metrolink were established on the site of the former carriage sidings at Queens Road. This location gave access to the Manchester to Bury electric line. The first part of the conversion entailed the closure of the railway between Victoria and Crumpsall in July 1991 and the introduction of a shuttle service of buses between the two stations which was extended to Bury when the electric trains were withdrawn completely on the 10 August and the whole of the Manchester to Bury railway became Metrolink property.

At Victoria station the Metrolink platforms were built on the area between the former platforms five to eight, a sharp curve enabled the new track to make a turn of 90 degrees to pass out of the train shed through a large hole cut in the south wall, crossing Long Millgate and Corporation Street before proceeding towards the city centre.

After several postponements Metrolink was opened between Victoria and Bury on the 6 April 1992 and from Victoria to the GMex centre on the 27th. GMex to Altrincham was opened on the 15 June and the final section from Piccadilly to Piccadilly station on the 20 July.

At the end of 1991 a scheme, as part of a bid to hold the Olympic Games in Manchester in the year 2000, was

Left upper: *Looking the worse for wear the bay platforms did not promise much for the future in 1981. Electric trains to Bury had been relocated to platforms 5 to 7 and the surplus siding lifted to make way for the planned Picc/Vic tunnel scheme which would have come to the surface at the south end of the suburban station.*

Left lower: *Although that part of the station near to the parcels office had been cleared the luggage bridge across the station still stands in 1993 also some of the columns which used to support the station roof.*

Opposite: *The Metrolink entered the station along the line of the old platforms 5 to 8 (upper) then curved sharply to the left parallel to the station concourse. It then passes (lower) through the wall of the station over what was the fish dock then Long Millgate and on its way to the city centre.*

announced to build a stadium which would hold 15,000 spectators on the site of platforms twelve to seventeen at Victoria and encompassing the area bound by Great Ducie Street, New Bridge Street, now renamed Trinity Way, Cheetham Hill Road and the railway along the line of platform twelve. In addition, on the land between Corporation Street and the Metrolink swallowing up what was left of Long Millgate, an hotel and multi-storey office block was planned. British Rail would reduce the station to four through tracks and two bay platforms adjacent to the Metrolink. At the end of December 1992 the whole of the station roof over platforms twelve to seventeen was removed together with the lines between platform eleven and twelve When the station was re-opened in 1993 trains used platforms fourteen to sixteen. In February the parcels office was demolished and a start was made to excavate the land between New Bridge Street and the railway. A temporary foot-bridge was erected at the Cheetham Hill Road end of the station to enable passengers to reached platform eleven when the subway was closed at the end of March.

The station became "open" on the 17 May when all the ticket barriers were removed, eighty years after they had first been erected by the LYR!

A new platform, built to take the place of platform twelve was brought into use on the 16 August and until the 15 November trains used platforms eleven, twelve, fifteen and sixteen. On that date all

traffic was concentrated on platforms eleven and twelve and work started to remove all traces of the 1884 station extension.

Two new platforms were opened on the 25 April 1994 when all the platforms were renumbered. The two bay platforms became one and two and the four through platforms became three to six. To distinguish between British Rail and Metrolink the latter

platforms are lettered A, B and C. Unfortunately, on the first day of opening the new platforms two vehicles of a freight train passing through platform six were derailed severely damaging the coping stones of the platform edge for most of its length preventing its use in the near future.

On Saturday 15 June 1996 a terrorist bomb exploded in the centre of Manchester about 400 yards from Victoria station. The

subsequent blast blew out many windows in the 1844 Hunts Bank station building and the 1909 office block, much of the glass from the latter building fell on to the ornamental canopy covering the pavement below. Very quickly the station was closed and included within an exclusion zone that was thrown around the city centre. Metrolink services were terminated at Picadilly and those from Bury at Woodlands Road station. A few days after the explosion passengers were allowed into the station using the New Bridge Street (Trinity Way) entrance and general access to the station was resumed on Thursday, 20 June. Apart from the windows there appeared to be no structural damage. The pavement canopy was cordoned off and supported with scaffolding poles but it was not until four years later that the canopy was renovated and brought back, as near as possible, to its original condition.

Left upper and centre: *Following the arrival of the Metrolink upgrading by repainting, new tiled flooring together with modern kiosks was undertaken to improve the station's appearance.*

Left lower: *The LYR frequently used mosaic panels above station amenities. The first class restaurant and refreshment room next to the grill room were prime examples.*

Opposite uper: *The effects of the blast from the explosion in the city centre in 1996 caused much damage to the front of the station building. Many windows were blown out with much of the glass falling onto the glass canopy along the pavement destroying that as well. The canopy was eventually reconstructed along with the clock face.*

Opposite lower: *At the northern side of the booking office is the surviving wall map of the original two showing the LYR system. It and the war memorial below still attract considerable interest.*

Late in 1997 the site of Red Bank carriage sidings was utilised as a works depot for re-signalling which was to be centred on Victoria station, with a state of the art signalling centre adjacent to Salford Crescent station. In July 1998 all the former LYR signal cabins which were still in operation, including the three electric cabins at Victoria, were closed and demolished very shortly afterwards. East Junction signal cabin, built in 1962, was pulled down early in 1999.

In the early morning of the 9 May 2003 some of the glass panels of the station roof gave way and crashed down to the platform below. The Metrolink platform A and the railway platforms 1 and 2, together with the car park were closed off. A report in August found that to repair the roof more than one million pounds would have to be raised since apart from the roof structure itself, a complex system of scaffolding would also have been needed to prevent disruption of both railway and Metrolink services.

Right: *Changes continue at the foot of the incline outside Victoria station. The Metrolink trains will continue to use the former electrified lines and the crossover will be retained to gain access to the outside world. The south, or slow, lines will be reduced to a single track beneath the Cheetham Hill Road bridge before dividing into the two bay platforms. The original through lines will remain passing through platforms three and four though the connection with the Loop Line has been taken out. The northern pair of tracks are also retained passing through platforms five and six,. Very soon, however, the connection with the Loop fast line will be severed. At the west end of the station amid tons of concrete the four tracks curve away past the site of Exchange station towards Salford leaving the old foot bridge standing in splendid isolation.*